Our Women

CHAPTERS ON THE SEX-DISCORD

BY
ARNOLD BENNETT

NEW YORK
GEORGE H. DORAN COMPANY

PRINTED IN THE UNITED STATES OF AMERICA

Publishing Statement:

This important reprint was made from an old and scarce book.

Therefore, it may have defects such as missing pages, erroneous pagination, blurred pages, missing text, poor pictures, markings, marginalia and other issues beyond our control.

Because this is such an important and rare work, we believe it is best to reproduce this book regardless of its original condition.

Thank you for your understanding and enjoy this unique book!

CONTENTS

INTRODUCTION: THE PERILS OF WRITING ABOUT WOMEN

INTRODUCTION

THE PERILS OF WRITING ABOUT WOMEN

THIS book is written by a man; there is no pretence that it is written by a hermaphrodite, asexual or inhuman being, or even by a superhuman individual who, through the favour of Heaven and a detached intelligence, has freed himself from the prejudices incident to sex.

Discord exists between the sexes. It always has existed, and it always will. (By which statement I do not mean to support the ridiculous maxim that human nature never changes. Human nature develops continually. The amœba, the simplest, one-celled form of life, is what human nature once was, and no break can be found in the chain of evolution which connects the two.) These chapters are an expression of the discord between the sexes. The impulse to write them springs from a sense of the discord, and, surely, could spring from nothing else. The idea would not occur to me to write a book about men; the subject would insufficiently attract me, because it would contain no challenging possibilities, I should as soon think of writing about the multiplication table.

Further, I have no hope or desire to resolve the discord, to establish harmony and put an end to the vast altercation. The altercation is fundamental and eternal. My object is merely to assist a little in the development of the altercation. For, just as human nature develops, so does the sex-discord develop. The plane of it shifts. (Personally, I believe that the plane rises.) A misconception or a misunderstanding is removed —only to be succeeded by another. New vistas of more subtle conflict are constantly being revealed.

The speculative have surmised that life, and presumably some rudiment of sex, moved upon the earth a hundred million years ago. Those who have acquainted themselves with the phenomena of somewhat more recent periods are prepared to assert that men and women strongly resembling ourselves lived and loved a quarter of a million years ago. Who would deny that the sex-discord then was cruder than to-day? But it may be considered fantastic to go even so far back. Let us take a modern woman such as the scriptural Rebekah, who was sitting at eve by the palm-shaded well only a few thousand years ago, and whose charm evidently raised up longings in the austere heart of Matthew Arnold only yesterday. Rebekah, with all her tranquillity, must have felt the sex-discord, but it positively was not the discord that agitates to-day, for example, a woman novelist united in love and matrimony to a man of science. Why, the sex-discord has noticeably developed since Coventry Patmore wrote "The Angel in the House"!

And who wants the sex-discord to be resolved? The sex-discord may be the most exasperating thing in existence, but it is by general agreement the most delightful and the most interesting. Its development by the devilish adventurousness of mankind is part of the great search for truth—and perhaps the best part. The philosopher seeks truth, but unless he knows he will not find it he is not a philosopher. If he really hoped to arrive at final truth, and if he possessed sagacity and self-control, he would abandon the quest in horror; for he would perceive that he was endangering the very foundation of the will to live. Truth is perfection. Life is a movement from imperfection towards perfection. Perfection is the end of life. It is equal to death.

And, mystics and seers notwithstanding, there is nothing so bad as death. If men and women were to wake one morning in perfect mutual comprehension and in the assurance that no discord separated them, on that day politics, even international politics, would cease to have significance. The sun where it shone—would shine in vain. The globe would put up its shutters. The sublime adventure would be over. And the First Cause would have to set to and think of something fresh.

Mention of the categories to which I have referred above—novelist (example of the artist), man of science, philosopher—recalls the terrible misgiving and diffidence that clouded the inception of this book in my mind. For the chapters, most absurdly, in spite of the author's wish, began by presenting themselves to me in a philosophic and even a scientific aspect.

I thought of the preparations which a man of science or a philosopher would have made had he undertaken a "monograph"—it would surely have been called a "monograph"—upon this my subject. In the first place, his mind would have been prepared for the task by a lifetime's discipline. His mind would be already an instrument trained by long habit in the methods best calculated to reach truth by the shortest way, which to the inexpert often seems the longest way. He would never argue from particulars to generals, never trust his emotions, never confuse prejudice with conviction, never indulge in the acrobatics of jumping to a conclusion, never lose sight of the great fact that everything in the universe is affected by everything else in the universe. He would always be deliberate, he would always test an inference, always suspect appearances, and always treat a mere impression with contumely. And wit and fancy he would abhor. Then, before starting, he would dissect the subject into divisions; he would draw out a few charts, and he would acquaint himself broadly with the conclusions arrived at by previous investigators.

From this point plans of work would differ with different men. Thus Darwin, if he had been in my place, would certainly have obtained a Government steamer and visited every port in the world where women were to be found. For, note, it would have been useless to tell Darwin that his subject was confined to Anglo-Saxon women. Darwin would have replied to such a shallow suggestion with the incontrovertible answer that women, like snakes, must be studied comparatively, and that to inquire into Anglo-Saxon women without inquiring into the women of Peru and the women of the Stone Age, would be obvious folly. He would have gone forth in the ship—and not a woman on board!—and in five years he would have returned with many volumes of classified notes. He would then (unless he forgot) have made a tour of England and more notes, and in another ten years he would have produced his monograph, which would have been translated into Italian and would have caused a prodigious ferment in Italy long before England had begun to surmise that a son of hers had once again cut a new path for the truth-seekers of all nations.

Herbert Spencer, the philosopher, would have acted quite otherwise. He would not have read anything. He would have taken the train to Brighton, and, having exhaustively examined the lodgings of Brighton for drains, southern aspect, furniture, food and heating apparatus, he would have engaged rooms to suit his temperament, and would have enjoined the landlady never to speak to him until he spoke to her. Then he would have engaged an educated woman of sedate respectability and unexciting figure to read to him about women, and he would have stopped her in the middle of any book and ordered her to begin another book. Then he would have banished all books as futile, and probably the reader also, and would have retired into his own brain; and, starting from some axiom of which the contrary was inconceivable, and binding himself by a rule never to assume anything of which the contrary was not inconceivable, he would very slowly, and with ample intervals for mental repose, have constructed in his brain and from the material of his brain a complete and flawless theory of Anglo-Saxon women. He would have had to pay for the printing of his own book, which would have involved him in financial loss; and the ultimate result would have been that no respectable philosopher or man of science in the future would dare to tackle the subject of women without having read Herbert Spencer thereon.

Now, when I contrasted my state and method with the state and method of these great investigating constructive thinkers, I had the right to be apprehensive; and the diffidence which seized me will be understood. Like most imaginative writers, I have read little, and in the main only for pleasure. My book knowledge of the physics of woman was, and is, limited to vague memories of certain manuals. I never could get through the work of Heinrich Keisch. I never read a word of Havelock Ellis on the matter. Yea, can it be said that I finished Ovid? I probably do not know even the names of the greatest writers about women. I have studied not one system of psychology. I have not travelled farther west than Chicago nor farther east than Rome, nor farther north than Stockholm nor farther south than Biskra. As for method, I have none. I am entirely incapable of organised research. To verify quotations is repugnant to me. I adore "particulars" and consider that one "particular" is quite sufficient material for so abstract and poor a thing as a "general." I dare say that I hold the record for the long jump to conclusions. I live by impressions and emotions. I am not averse from prejudices when they suit my enterprise. If convictions for inaccuracy involved penal servitude I should have passed my whole existence in prison. I have no exact knowledge on any subject whatever.

I decided that before writing this book I must make an honest effort to remedy my enormous incapacity for the business. But later, coming gradually to my senses, I decided that I must attempt no such idiotic and impossible thing, and that what was chiefly wrong was not my incapacity (though that was wrong enough), but my conception of the business in front of me. I perceived that it would be just as wise for me to try to write a "monograph" as it would have been for Herbert Spencer to try to write a novel or a comedy. I perceived further—what must be plain to every enlightened reader—that as art is not the whole of life, so philosophy and science are not the whole of life, but that life is a very mighty and inclusive affair.

And, still further, I perceived that even at their own game philosophers and men of science are imperfect. For example, all the few works of philosophy and science with which I am acquainted are plainly corrupted by emotion and prejudice, and by the wish, however slight, to prove something which the author has settled in advance ought to be true. Indeed, some famous works of philosophy and science may fitly be compared to bad novels.

Again, I have noticed that great thinkers, when they enter a region which I have explored, are apt to become absurd. Bernard Shaw disproving the genius of Shakespeare is not more comic than Spencer when, in the "Introduction to the Study of Sociology," he indisputably demonstrates that first-class stylists, such as Addison, really didn't understand how to write. And I can imagine Spencer enjoyably tearing to pieces Keats's dictum that beauty is truth, truth beauty, and that we need naught else. Yet Keats's dictum will possibly hold the field long after Spencer has sunk to be nothing but a name in a dictionary. And if Spencer had in fact composed a monograph on women, what a horrid mess he would have made of it! And how it would have been vitiated by the influence upon him of George Eliot, the one woman whose glance penetrated the armour of his steel-clad heart!

But I would not decry the majestic workers in philosophy and science. And if I tease them it is because I venerate them. Indeed, my tendency is, when I reflect upon the method of these men, to think that no other method than theirs is worthy to be practised. Such, however, is not the case. The progress of mankind has need of every method that is sincere and instinctive, and none should be ashamed of the method to which he was born. The world owes much to Bacon and Newton, but not more than to Wordsworth and Dr. Johnson—or even Charles Lamb. And is it not notorious that the most successful prophets have been, not men of science and scholars, but men of letters? Burke, who was a prejudiced, oratorical and hysterical writer, and whose knowledge of history Macaulay and Stubbs would have scorned, somehow acquired a juster notion of the trend of Europe than any of your scientific omniscient historians. There is room, in the thick crowd of truth-seekers, for honest people who, lacking the qualities fundamental in a philosopher and a man of science, yet share with them the quality of imagination and possess other qualities generally denied by nature to philosophers and men of science. Everybody may help.

And there is a special excuse for the unscientific and the unphilosophic if they dare to deal with the subject which I have chosen. Philosophers and men of science leave it alone. These latter seem not to be attracted by what I will call the human dailiness of life. The man of science is more likely to investigate the daily habits and polity of the wasps which fly in at his windows in summer, searching for jam, than the daily habits and polity of the human beings who are intimately sharing with him the adventure of life. And if he is drawn to the study of men and women, they will, a hundred to one, be the men and women who lived long since. And if he is drawn to the study of contemporary men and women he will only examine them in their mass-aspects, or, at any rate, in only a single aspect of their multitudinous manifestation.

As for contemporary women, he has too frequently either avoided them in a regrettable cowardice or an equally regrettable disdain, or has conducted his sexual relations with gross clumsiness and deplorable lack of comprehension. Titans of intellect whose labours influence the destiny of the human race have never kissed, and when confronted with a pretty woman have not known what on earth to do, and could not manage a pouting wife at supper to save their souls.

It is true that artists, too, have been very maladroit with women. But they have seldom or never avoided women. Artists have always been in love with actuality, and with the women about them as the most striking phenomena in actuality. Actuality seems to be too trifling and accidental for philosophers and men of science, or it may be that, with the humility characteristic of the greatest truth-seekers, they are intimidated by its maddening changeful complexity. Perhaps philosophers and men of science are right.

Perhaps they achieve more beneficent results by ignoring actuality. Perhaps their method is unsuited to the study of it; and the other method, the impressionist, fanciful, unscientific, wayward, leaping, philosophically indefensible method, my method, may be the proper one for the range of subjects that includes mine. For myself, I think that it is the only method for my subject that anybody with a sense of humour would or could employ.

Artists produce their work out of their own experience—and usually out of the experience which comes to them, not the experience which consciously they go forth to seek. Even when an artist writes a historical novel, or paints a historical picture, the history is merely a fancy costume for his personal experience of life. Now, every man has had some fundamental experience of women. Most have had a great deal. Some have had too much. All have arrived at a definite attitude towards women. All are in possession of a genuine philosophy of women. Millions of men go to the grave without having reached definite individual conclusions on hundreds of really important subjects. But woman is never among these neglected subjects. The mention of women will instantly give vitality and conviction to the most lackadaisical and perfunctory masculine conversation. The misogynist shows all the time that women obsess him. The man whom circumstance has cut off from direct intercourse with women will construct his theories of them from seeing and hearing them in the street, in cafés, in the theatre, in church and chapel. In short, all men are full of interesting matter concerning women. It is said that every man has the stuff in him of one good novel. I doubt it; but I do not deny that every man has the stuff in him of one original book about women. And why more men—even philosophers and scientists—do not write books about women, and more women books about men, I cannot imagine.

In this affair, all that applies to the ordinary man applies in a considerably greater degree to the artist, because, as a rule, he sees more of women, draws them more to himself, uses them more, and, despite his responsiveness and susceptibility, is less liable to be hoodwinked. Indeed, fewer women deceive artists than are deceived by them. A man not an artist will often sacrifice everything for a woman; and such a man—like a rake, but for a different reason—is the last person whose estimate of women should be trusted. But an artist will very seldom sacrifice his art for a woman. He will much more probably employ her, with an astounding ruthlessness in the service of his art. A woman has no greater rival than the art of an artist; and the jealousy between one woman and another is mild in comparison with the jealousy which may animate a woman against the art of the artist who has captured her. Indeed, artists are in a unique position of advantage. Their detachment is terrible. Women know it. Hence the conclusions of artists about women are presumably entitled to a particular consideration, since destiny has favoured them doubly—in experience and in the instinct for expression.

Two perils, however, beset the path of anybody whose mind is not scientifically trained (and especially the artist), who would treat of this subject which has intimidated philosophers and men of science. The first springs from the tendency to despise science and the method thereof. The artist often, if not generally, regards science as opposed to him, as the negation of his ideals and destructive of freedom and the emotions. Such an attitude is ridiculous; it is babyish and rooted in a shameful ignorance. Every great man of science has something of the artist in his composition; he has been an apostle of freedom, and emotion scarcely distinguishable from the emotion of the artist has inspired his work. If any artist doubts this, let him read the closing pages of Herbert Spencer's disquisition on the Unknowable; or the preface to Dr. Johnson's Dictionary—which, after all, is in the nature of a scientific treatise.

And, similarly, every artist should also have in him something of the scientist, a rocky foundation upon which he can build safely. An artist may be as wild and capricious as he chooses. He may blow where he listeth. He may assert with the utmost conviction: "This that I do is interesting only because it is an expression of me." He may depend on impressions, and the impressions may be the impressions of a genius. He may decline to relate himself to anything that has gone before or is likely to come after. He may be persuaded that he is the absolute. An immense creative force may be his. But if that which he accomplishes is valuable and permanent it will be found to be pervaded by some scientific conception; it will have form and idea, both of which are more the offspring of science than of art.

Artists commonly do not study ideas; they mysteriously absorb them; but they cannot absorb unless they are sympathetic to them. Tennyson was not a student; Balzac certainly was not. Neither of them could have come without confusion through an examination upon the scientific and philosophic ideas of his time. Some of their answers in such an examination would have been "howlers" of the most pleasing kind. But they had absorbed great principles, and these principles, consciously or unconsciously, guided them with credit through the labyrinth of their way-wardness as artists. So much so that they became interpreters and illustrators of science to the profane.

Let not, therefore, the artist who takes upon himself to discuss women imagine that he can with impunity conduct himself as if science did not exist. He cannot. On the other hand, he need not be afraid of science in the manner of some artists who are too diffident to despise it. Science is not a thing apart. There is no dividing line between ordinary knowledge and scientific knowledge. Science, according to one of the most perfect descriptions ever devised, is merely "organised common sense." And in so far as anyone organises his common sense he is scientific.

The other peril lies in the temptation to make points. There is no subject on earth in which the temptation to make points is more powerful, the reward in joyous applause more generous and more sure, and the resulting falsification of truth more pitiful, than the subject of women when it is handled by men. The same thing, though in a less degree, may be asserted of the subject of men when it is handled by women. But women have fewer public opportunities than men of making sport of the opposite sex, and a smaller gift of humour and wit to help them in the facile and showy enterprise.

In conversation, at the play, in books and newspapers, at the banquet and the lecture and the meeting, the most banal cynical generalisation, the feeblest quip, the crudest aphorism upon this sovereign subject is certain to raise a laugh—a laugh in which women themselves will join as heartily as men. More cheap renown has been achieved by facetiousness and cynicism about women than by anything in the whole realm of social controversy. The biggest fool or rascal ever born can achieve a name in this field if only he is silly enough or unscrupulous enough.

And—what is more subtly disturbing—the subject seems to be a very forcing bed of wit and humour; I mean real wit and humour. All writers on social topics, from him who wrote "Ecclesiasticus" and him who wrote Shakespeare down to Meredith and Oscar Wilde, appear at their most engaging and brilliant when performing variations on this theme. And lesser men have climbed to immortality thereby who would otherwise surely have fallen into oblivion. The mischief is that a very great deal of what is said is at least half true, little of it is quite untrue, and a considerable proportion of it is as true as any human utterance can hope to be.

And yet truth, as I have said, is pitifully falsified. It is falsified because one sex, not both, comes in for nearly all the criticism. You may take a long series of statements, and every statement may be undeniable, and still you may disseminate a vast untruth. Women are no doubt as full of defects as the wit of man has for centuries announced. But the wit of man has never to the same extent put itself to the trouble of displaying the defects of men. It would be possible to take the greatest saint alive and by accurately cataloguing his trespasses to show him a perfect prodigy of sin. He would still be a saint.

"Ah!" you may exclaim. "But men can be generous in appreciation of women!"

They can. They are. They are too frequently too generous. They rarely praise women without spilling over into sentimentality and even gush. They will make sport for hours, and then they will say: "The women! God bless 'em!" Loud applause. But a different sort of applause, an applause which is less a compliment to women than a reassuring salve to the conscience of men who feel that they have been too witty.

The broad conclusion of all this is that before the public women have been unfairly treated, in that they have been subjected to an ordeal to which men have not been subjected. The right course for the future is that no man should allow himself a witticism against women until he has perpetrated a witticism against men. Indeed, to redress the balance somewhat, he should be compelled to make two or two dozen witticisms against men as a preliminary to one witticism against women.

Mind, I do not assert offhand that women are not more imperfect than men, and that men would not emerge more creditably than women from an ordeal similar to that which the structure of society has forced upon women. It might be so. It might not be so. All I assert is that there is nothing in the published record to prove that it would be so.

Fairness is in every man, if he will seek it. And every man, deep in his heart, knows what he really thinks. It specially behoves every masculine discourser upon women to seek the fairness which is in him, to get down to the honest bedrock of his thought, and to remember always that in this matter, though the reward of false witness is alluring and immense, false witness is still the same old iniquity.

One thing is sure, namely, that social customs have had the effect of exaggerating the differences between men and women. A sagacious woman, Lady Mary Wortley Montagu, a woman so independent that though she kept always on excellent terms with her husband and her family she managed generally to live about a thousand miles from them, wrote to her married daughter a wise saying about the sexes, and she wrote it in the fullness of experience towards the end of her life:

"I have never in all my various travels seen but two sorts of people, *and those very like one another;* I mean men and women. . . ."

CHAPTER ONE: CHANGE IN LOVE

CHAPTER ONE

CHANGE IN LOVE

WHEN man was annoyed, his mind ranged over his experience and he invented the maxim: All women are alike. It is true, but it is no more true than that all men are alike. In so far as Abraham Lincoln was like the madman Wilkes Booth who shot him, all women may be said to be alike. Women differ as much as pearls—of course! My reason for so crudely pointing this out is that when I generalise about women, I do not usually intend my generalisations to apply to all women or even to most women. At present I have in view women of the top class and of those classes which admittedly imitate the top (or leisured) class; and I am excluding women of the bottom class, that is to say, the largest class, which in the harsh adventurousness and precariousness of its daily existence has a set of ideals of its own, and which never attempts to imitate the top class save spasmodically in superficial trifles.

Ignoring, therefore, the majority of mankind, let us examine one aspect of the relations between men and women in the period which by common consent has just closed. We shall be talking of that which was, not of that which is; so that we may permit ourselves some freedom of speech.

In the top class, the class which had succeeded and which set the tone, why did the average man marry? Can it be said that he married mainly in order to have children and to continue or establish a family tradition? It cannot. The desire for children persists, but a growing perception of the conveniences and comforts incident to not having children began long ago to weaken the desire for children. The change may be expressed thus: Formerly parents had children without taking thought. Latterly they had children only by deliberate intention. Nor can it be said that men as a rule married in order to provide a mitigation of the solitude and the maladies which otherwise would render them miserable in old age. Young and youngish men do not look so far ahead.

It would be less untrue to say that men were influenced to marry by the felt need of a housekeeper and minister for practical domestic affairs. They wanted an independent establishment and they wanted somebody to look after it. But this explanation of marriage is exceedingly partial, and the percentage of truth in it can be put down as almost negligible. For in the top class men did not demand any practical domestic expertness whatever in their prospective wives, and no regular educational machinery existed for giving to prospective wives a technical knowledge in the wife's sphere at all comparable to the technical knowledge of the husband in the husband's sphere.

The classes immediately below, and indeed considerably below, the top class followed their leaders in this matter. And it was quite customary for a clerk whose physical comfort depended on the sound housekeeping of his wife to marry a girl without the slightest assurance that she was capable of cooking a joint, or of distinguishing between fresh and unfresh fish in a shop, or of cleaning paint, or of ensuring that anybody else could efficiently do these things for her. As for the man in the top class, his next act after choosing a wife was to choose a housekeeper possessing the technical knowledge which his wife lacked, and it is ten to one that he would have resented such technical knowledge in a spouse. He would have said to himself: "The girl is too efficient—there must be something not quite nice about her."

Hence we arrive at the conclusion that man in the period just closed must have married largely in order to have a companion. (It was a good reason, the best reason, especially as the desire for a companion often includes the desire to cherish and protect a companion.) And girls were brought up to be companions to men, though in a far less degree, and with far less seriousness, than, say, the Japanese mousmée. But man did not want a female companion all day. In fact he deliberately separated himself from her during what were to him the most important hours of the day; and during those hours she had to devote herself to what was evidently the other main function of her career. She had to prove to the world by ocular demonstration, that her man had the means to keep a woman in luxury and idleness. Luxury and idleness were still in theory the ideals of the fine world. Man himself had discovered that excessive luxury was apt to be a bore, and that idleness was assuredly exasperation; but the ideals remained, and he achieved and illustrated them vicariously, through his wife. The wife was the living, moving proof that the husband had succeeded. Her prime duty in the hours of companionship, as in the other hours, was to exist with charm, expensiveness, and futility.

Thus the destiny and honour of woman was to be parasitic. And if circumstances in the early years of womanhood forced her not to be parasitic her aim was nevertheless to become parasitic as soon as possible and as completely as possible. Among women there was always a competition for men. And if there were enough men to go round, there was still competition for the best men, that is, for the men best able to fulfil for women the acknowledged ideal of perfect parasitism. In this competition general inefficiency was at a premium and futility was at a premium. The hours of companionship were the man's hours of relaxation and repose; and in such hours a man does not want too much seriousness. Therefore the things of the mind took second place, and the whole plane of intercourse was lower than under another system it might have been. The reaction was wide; it affected man through woman, and all society was affected. The intelligence of woman was frustrated, and her conscience dulled, by the great design of display, parade, intentional waste, and exquisite futility; and even the exercise of her charm was impaired and shamed because it was confined mainly to the charm of the body.

Mental indolence is a stimulant of the grosser senses, which in the period now ended were further titillated and excited by a social atmosphere that was characterised beyond anything else by physical luxury.

With woman, nearly all effort towards self-realisation ceased at the age of eighteen or nineteen. Henceforward her aim was to exchange one form of parasitism (if, as usually happened, she was already a parasite) for another form of parasitism more agreeable to her. Having reached that other form, she found herself more deeply than ever entangled in the mesh of the senses. Her chief device in the struggle for individuality was the exploitation of her bodily charm, and her ultimate weapon was the caress. If she loved—and she did love—her only genuine work was a work of preparation for the return of the man to her in the evening. If she did not love, she had no genuine work which would not clash with the received ideal. The result upon the complexion of society was inevitable. We glossed it over with a thousand sentimentalities; but it was there plain enough.

Of course women, the base creatures, acquiesced in the system. The shocking truth is that, speaking broadly, they rather liked it. For if human beings enjoy being energetic, they also enjoy sloth—and perhaps are inclined to regard the use of energy primarily as a means to sloth. And that the majority of sophisticated and normal people enjoy some luxury cannot be disputed. The ascetic would like his hair-shirt delicately embroidered. Women were made to understand by their physical and economic superiors that the way to luxury, for them, was not the hard climb of effort but the soft descent through indolence and futility. They were tempted—and the temptation was a command. They gradually fell. It was very naughty of them. They well deserved the constant reprehension and disdain which men, always so magnanimous, bestowed upon them for having yielded to the enticement that was more than half a menace. Who can deny that men, similarly situated, would have behaved more nobly? For is it not notorious that men, when tempted by the flesh, always put away the allurement with a grand masculine gesture?

The period which I have described is now closed. Some will say, and say with anger, that there never was any such period, and that my description is a mere travesty of the past. I admit that my description is very incomplete; but I did not start out to tell the whole truth—indeed, the whole truth about the relations of men and women will probably never be known, and certainly will never be written. I expressly confined myself to one aspect of those relations. I do, however, assert that that aspect was the principal aspect, and that the colour of it deeply affected all the other aspects—even the most beautiful and touching. The conditions which I have set down were fundamental, and it was against such conditions that certain women, in concert with certain men, revolted.

The conditions were not imaginary. They were so real that they positively infuriated women who hate waste of good material—in particular when the good material happens to be human. And these women were so antagonised by the accepted ideals of womanliness that they attempted to cast, not some of them, but all of them, aside. Happily the attempt failed, as it was bound to do; and the discovery has now been made that personal charm and elegant shoes and visits to the manicurist can successfully go with extreme independence and anti-parasitism.

The war between the old and the new ideals is not yet over, though it is won. I pretended, for the sake of ease in speech, that the old period is finished and cut off. It is not. You have only to reflect, for example, upon the astonishing public importance given to what are delicately known as "undies" to perceive that it is not. Periods of human evolution never are cut off. They merge into one another, like colours in the rainbow, and nobody can tell where one ends and where the next begins. Still, a definite and decisive advantage has been gained by the new ideals. The other war (that which opened in Belgium) gave tremendous assistance to the new ideals, especially in Britain; but it by no means created them, and they would have conquered anyhow, for the mere reason that they appeal irresistibly to commonsense and to the sense of justice. The decisive advantage is this: that it is no longer quite correct for a truly proper and unexceptionable woman not to have something to do apart from her husband and her house.

When I say "something" I mean something beyond the ordinary charity business. The ordinary charity business, which is at bottom little but the officious patronising of the poor at no sacrifice by the rich, has always been the resource of truly proper and unexceptionable women ever since the days of "Lady Bountiful," who must have been an odious creature. It was a marvellous dope for an inconvenient conscience. It is less marvellous now. Women, in order to be correct, have to go beyond it, or to make a pretence of doing so. And herein is the great gain to the cause of the future. The lady-representatives of the past made an irretrievable false move when they allowed their curiosity to drive them to visit, as sightseers, the institutions in which the lady-representatives of the future were actually at work. The two sets of ideals met then in the flesh; they no doubt hated each other with a high moral hatred (as was excusable and even right), but the genuine scorn was all on one side; and the past which had come (once more) to patronise, went away patronised.

The mysterious workings of the collective conscience of the community were well illustrated by an incident in the married life of that well-known couple, Jack and Jill, which occurred only the day before yesterday. Jill, as is shown by her early history, was of the old-fashioned variety of woman. Jack had a good commercial position. It was perhaps modest, but it held fine possibilities, and already Jack was proving to the world his ability to keep a woman in idleness and in a little more than the luxury customary to their station. Jill's ambition was satisfied. She had wanted to be a parasite and she was a parasite. She loved; she was loved. She was happy; Jack was happy. She had nothing left to hope for except Jack's gradual advancement, which was a certainty. Here in fact was the ancient ideal achieved.

Jack came home one night a quarter of an hour late. She enquired about his business in the carefully genial tone in which a woman (or a man) enquires about a rival.

"And what have *you* been doing?" asked Jack when he had rendered his account.

"Oh! I've been very busy," said she.

"I'm sure you have," said Jack quickly.

"You know, I've really a great deal to do; I never have a minute," said she.

"Oh! I know," said Jack, once more in eager agreement.

And all was seemingly well in their caresses and their security and their correctness and their justifiable complacency. Each pretended that the collective conscience was not steadily burrowing under the foundations of the beautiful structure of their lives and threatening the high towers of correctness and complacency. But the collective conscience was burrowing nevertheless. And one night Jill said to Jack:

"You know Ada is very reliable with baby."

And another night Jill said:

"I hear they want someone as superintendent of the Economic Circle rooms—someone who is responsible and can see to things. Mrs. Beechinor asked me whether I could take it on. I laughed"—Jill gave a nervous laugh as she said that she laughed—"I told the great Mrs. B. that it was *quite* out of the question for me. For one thing, you have to understand card-indexing yourself if you're to keep the library girl in order, and then it means one night a week, besides five afternoons. And I couldn't possibly be away from home at night, could I? But of course that's not the point. I've always got enough to do here, haven't I? It isn't as if I had any time to spare."

And Jack replied:

"Of course not."

But Jack knew, and Jill knew also, that the bulk of Jill's day was passed in activities which were merely invented in order to enable her to assert that she was occupied, and that even when she was engaged in what she called improving her mind she was really engaged in waiting for him to come home. How delightful to think that a woman is waiting for your footstep!

And one night Jill said:

"It appears you can learn all about card-indexing in about a month."

And Jack said, with an air of agreeable interest:

"Oh! Is that so?"

And Jill said:

"Of course I daresay I *could* find time, if I squeezed things in a bit. But then there's the evening a week. I couldn't think of leaving you alone, darling, after your hard day."

"Oh! I should be all right," says he.

"Naturally I shouldn't do it for the money," says she.

"Why not?" says he. "The money would be your own, and I expect you'd know what to do with it."

Jill took the place. Jack could no longer feel the sensuous secret thrill due to the fact that a beloved woman was waiting, waiting all day for him to return, living solely for him and in him and on him. Yet his spirits rose, and hers too. There was a change in the air of their home. It was as though the air had received an extra charge of oxygen. Jack was as proud of Jill's post as Jill herself. He mentioned it in that falsely casual tone that always signifies intense satisfaction. The collective conscience, appeased, stopped burrowing. In other words the spectres of waste and futility had been exorcised. Security and complacency were firmly re-established. Jack's business ceased in Jill's eyes to be her rival. She talked to Jack as one worker to another. She knew what life was. She clung less; she caressed less; and Jack perceived that he was less like an oak and a sultan than in the past. But the gestures with which Jill returned from her evening spell were ravishing, and more than atoned for Jack's partial loss of the sensation of being an oak and a sultan. . . .

Take, now, the Jack and Jill of the future —and of the not far distant future. Jill is professionally the pilot of an aeroplane. Of course there was a considerable amount of trouble before Jills obtained the right to pilot aeroplanes. There always is trouble when

Jills try to do what no previous Jills have done. When, for example, a Jill began to copy Jack's bad habit of smoking, she could at first only smoke under pain of being unsexed—theoretically. To-day, after much turmoil, all Jills throughout the world may smoke in the homes over which they preside, and still remain within the bounds of social correctness. In some countries they may correctly smoke in restaurants, in some not. In some countries they may correctly smoke in railway carriages. But in no country may they smoke on the top of a public vehicle, such as an omnibus or a tramcar, save at the serious risk of forfeiting the respect of mankind.

The Jill of the future met similar difficulties in the matter of flying. It was held first that she simply could not pilot an aeroplane. And then it was held that if she could and did she would be (*a*) depriving Jack of his bread, (*b*) unsexing herself, (*c*) making discord between the sexes, (*d*) ruining the institution of the family, (*e*) endangering the true progress of the whole human race. Still, she did fly; none of the terrible prophecies was fulfilled; and the earth sedately revolved as usual.

Well, after a day spent in manœuvring a huge machine a hundred and fifty feet wide and a hundred feet long, Jill comes down to earth, gives orders to a cohort of mechanics, removes her leathern garments and attires herself in delicate and fine raiment for the evening with Jack. Jack is a print-seller, a great expert on etchings, drypoints, mezzotints, aquatints, engravings, and what not. He spends his days in a shop, catching occasional glimpses of the firmament through a somewhat obscure window.

Do you see Jack masculinely protecting Jill as they move along the pavement to the gay restaurant? Do you see him sagaciously guiding across the roadway this girl whose daily task it is to guide a flying machine through all the windy perils of the sky? Do you think she has anything to learn from him about keeping her nerve when they find themselves between two automobiles approaching in opposite directions? Do you imagine that she, with her high salary, is any the less likely than he is to pay for the dinner and the theatre? I don't.

And when they finally get back to the intimacy of home do you suppose that the recital of his day in the shop will be more impressive than the recital of her day in the clouds and in and out of the wind-pockets? Do you dream that when he kisses her the look in her eye and the acquiescence of her limbs will be precisely those of a sheltered girl whose heart is saying: "All day since you left me I have been living for this moment?" Do you deny that the duet or duel of tenderness will not be exceedingly modified from the duet or duel which our contemporary Jacks and Jills were wont to perform? It is obvious that the change will be striking.

You protest, however, that I have chosen an extreme example of new relations. I have, in order to illustrate graphically the disconcerting possibilities of the future. But the example is not so extreme, nor will it be so rare, as some of us may assume. And, moreover, there will be very numerous examples only less remarkable. And these examples will undoubtedly influence the general attitude of all members of one sex to all members of the other sex. It is certain that the mere increased activity of women, as well as the increased variety of that activity, must produce reactions, both mental and physical, in the inter-play of the sexes, which inter-play is probably about half of life. A real independence of women will help to put an end to that exasperating exercise of factitious power to which women were, and still are, driven by the thwarted human instinct for self-assertion. Jill will no longer ask Jack to do things that are patently absurd and then, when he demands her reason, reply with finality: "Because I want you to." And in general all those sinister, underground and conspiratorial methods of Jill—methods which were no doubt perfectly natural to her condition but which Jack has patronisingly regarded as entirely irrational and inexcusable—will tend to disappear.

But the greatest development will be seen in a new phase of the phenomenon of love. The character of love is bound to alter. In regard to love and all that appertains to it, women have hitherto been in a state approaching morbidity. They have had a vast deal too much leisure in which to brood over that matter; it was their main avenue of escape into some sort of freedom; and they were forced by circumstances to foster its material side at the expense of its spiritual side. The ideal of living only for love will have to vanish, and it ought to vanish. Undue reflection upon love, in conditions of futility and mental indolence, cannot fail to debase it into unhealthiness. Women whose days are interestingly and usefully full will have no time to be morbid. Their minds will be nourished. They will think more of their own minds and of men's minds, and less of their own bodies and of men's bodies. And men will assuredly be thereby led to do he same. The phenomenon of love will shed its superfluous grossness. Affection may be strengthened, but crude passion will diminish. And inclinations and habits will be modified accordingly.

An appreciable proportion of citizens will without doubt once again resent powerfully what I have just written. Some will cry out upon me that the prophecy is false. To which there is no immediate convincing answer. But others will accept the truth of the prophecy and hate it, and will exclaim, "I hope to heaven I shall be dead before that time comes, for life will not be worth living." The world has heard many such exclamations in its eventful history.

I should like to reassure the affrighted seekers after death and to persuade them to struggle on in the mortal coil. These sexual changes will not arrive suddenly. You will not wake up to-morrow morning and find them in being. You will have full opportunity to accommodate yourselves to them. Further, so long as women continue in physical inferiority and in their exclusive privilege of motherhood, no conceivable change can rob men of the great primary sensations peculiar to masculinity.

However, I would not put my trust in such secondary arguments. The master argument is that the human Odyssey on this planet has been an infinite series of astounding changes, and that its interestingness is as acute to-day as it ever was. Indeed, I venture to assert that its interestingness is more acute to-day than ever it was. We have always feared that the savour of life would be lost if things went on as they obviously were going on, and our fears have always been falsified. Who that is a parent will deny that his parents would have been horror-struck and ready to go out of business as parents could they have foreseen the terrible independence of modern children? Yet modern parents get quite as much satisfaction out of their children as any generation of parents ever did—and, I think, more.

Solomon himself would have shut up his seraglio and imitated Job in misfortune had he been confronted with the ladies of ancient Greece. Socrates and Plato would have taken lodgings in a Diogenes tub if they had been translated among the women of the eighteenth century. And the English squires and dames of the eighteenth century would have been laid low with a paralysis of shame at the mere thought of what women have done during the great war. Gifted with a vision of the future, each era would have confidently and miserably anticipated the end of true romance in the next era. Women have been unsexed a thousand times, and yet the unfathomable wonder of their sex survives most marvellously complete. The sex discord baffles and ravishes us. So it will be, whatever occurs. The Jack of fifty or a hundred years hence will look upon his Jill as the very quintessence of femininity. But he will look upon our Jills as a backward and a rather insipid crew, and upon the Jacks of 1920 as a race of males not emerged from the primitive sexual ideals of Orientalism.

CHAPTER TWO: THE ABOLITION OF SLAVERY

CHAPTER TWO

THE ABOLITION OF SLAVERY

THE economics of woman must begin with the girl; and yet most parents, even at this modern date, when common sense has made such ravages in the world's ancient sentimentality, hate to connect pounds, shillings and pence with the charming and innocent creature that is so mysteriously growing up in the house. All feel her strange power and attraction. Not only do the young men feel it who are already being drawn to the house by the magic spell; the parents feel it, just as freshly as though no girl had ever blossomed before in the whole history of mankind. And the young lady herself feels it; and let her be as naïve as you like—she privately exults in it. That is why upon occasion she will be so imperious and wilful and provocative. Can you watch the curve of the cheek and the fling of the head without somehow agreeing that it would be an outrage to give any hint in her presence as to the existence of vile, harsh economics? And so, in too many cases, the girl is kept apart from economics as from an infection or an undesirable acquaintance. Is not papa working hard for her? It not mamma daily inculcating into her the great principles which underlie goodness and attractiveness—especially attractiveness? Will not some thoroughly suitable male person come along soon and apply respectfully for the honour of taking papa's place as her shield and buckler?

The devoted parents seem not to understand that they are engaged in creating a slave. But they are nevertheless creating a slave to economics, whose rule will in the end infallibly assert itself. Chance, of course, may preserve the slave from the worst forms of civilised slavery; but, on the other hand, chance may not. Would the sagacious parent leave the fate of the beloved creature to chance? Well, apparently he would, though to do so is beyond doubt a crime. And still he can sleep comfortably at nights. Such is the force of tradition.

The father who plays the shield and buckler rôle exclusively is a criminal for various reasons. He is a criminal because he may die suddenly, and, in spite of a fine appearance of riches, leave his family without any adequate protection against the inexorable operation of economics. The thing has happened millions of times, bringing about that lamentable phenomenon, the "lady in distressed circumstances." And the father is a criminal because he may fall into reduced circumstances himself, without dying. And he is a criminal because the girl may marry and her husband die. And he is a criminal because nobody may want to marry the girl, or the girl may want to marry nobody. And he is a criminal because in these interesting years of transition anything may happen anywhere. In Russia there are girls who were tenderly screened from economics and who are now glad to sweep the streets for two roubles a day; they cannot sweep efficiently, but they cannot do any other job at all. In brief, the father is a criminal because he is sacrificing the girl's future to her present, or allowing her to sacrifice it.

"Let her be happy," says the affectionate criminal; but it is just as if he said in those doting tones: "Let her be unhappy."

The girl may enjoy the flowery path traced

for her by the criminal. The girl's own notions, however, are beside the point. The girl knows no better. . . . Yet sometimes in disconcerting glimpses she does know better. And probably there are few girls brought up solely to be ornamental and loving who have not experienced horrid transient qualms of impotence and humiliation in the midst of their brightest triumphs.

The great and terrible fact which girls do not and cannot imaginatively realise and which parental criminals can realise and do not, is that girls die young. Boys may live nearly for ever. I have known boys of sixty-six, in practically full possession of the weapons of boys. But few girls survive their thirtieth year. Herein is the gravest of all sex inequalities, and nothing will cure it—at any rate, in our day or in the next million years or so. After thirty another being has taken the place of the girl. The girl has natural weapons—weapons of remarkable quality, if very incomplete—but weapons which she cannot transmit to her successor. She may, however, provided her father is not a criminal, acquire other weapons, less brilliant but more durably effective, which certainly will be transmitted to her successor—reliable weapons against time, against bereavement, against a bad husband, against all manner of evil chance.

Probably no parent would say in words to a girl:

"My dear, as you are you have only one weapon to employ in the existence into which for my own stisfaction, I have brought you. In a few years this weapon will be useless. There are other weapons of knowledge and skill which might later on, when you have changed into another being who is not a girl, save you from misery and unhappiness. But I will not provide you with these because to acquire them would be rather a bore for you, and I like to see you care-free and gay, and full of illusions and ignorance, and defenceless. It is true that your entire future is thereby at best impaired and at worst ruined, but we will hope for happiness and trust to luck."

No parents would say such words; but actions speak louder than words, and the actions of millions of parents have given and still are giving precisely this message to the credulous creatures whom they cherish. It is unbelievable, but it is true. I perceive around me, even in the enlightened year 1920, multitudes of girls whose lives are being shaped according to that message. I meet them in beautiful frocks, amid scenes of joy, good taste, and luxury. They are polite to my grey hairs, and I delight in their company. But I am tempted to murmur to them: "Excuse me, but do you see that awful gulf right at your very feet?" Of course I murmur no such thing, because to do so would not be nice. At all costs I must be nice. Moreover, they would not excuse me. Therefore I ask them instead what they think of the Russian ballet or of the League of Nations or of the Labour situation or of the Lawn Tennis championships. This is human nature.

My point is that, in order to abolish the economic slavery of women, every girl ought to be able to earn her own living. Further, she ought for a period actually to earn as much money as would suffice to keep her in decency and independence if she had no other resources. To do this she must be brought at a comparatively early age into contact with the realities of the world. Call the realities ugly if you please. No reality is as dangerous as an illusion, and few are as ugly. If I could choose an epitaph for my grave it would be: "He tried to destroy illusions."

But in reply to my blunt point about girls and their livelihood I seem to hear you retorting:

"Of course! We are all agreed on that. You are stating a platitude. We expected something more interesting from you; for instance, some exquisite psychical analysis of the mentality of girls. *A quoi rêvent les jeunes filles?* And so on."

For me nothing is more interesting than the aforesaid point. It should come and does come before any psychical analysis. And what I have stated, if it is a platitude, is a platitude only of theory, not of practice. Look around; and deny it—if you have the nerve.

I have been material. But I will be still more material, for I would as soon be hung for a sheep as for a lamb. I will say further that, since the family is the natural and everlasting unit of social existence, and the well-being of the family is founded on the efficiency of the domestic machine, and women are the natural creators and controllers of the domestic machine—therefore all parents of girls ought to see that girls learn to manage the domestic machine from top to bottom in a thoroughly expert way, just as parents of boys see that boys learn to be lawyers or engineers or doctors or acrobats or plumbers. And if parents of girls don't do this, girls are quite alert and influential enough nowadays to see that parents do it and are themselves to blame if it is not done. And I say again that the inefficiency of the average genteel domestic machine is a serious factor in the inefficiency of the national machine, and that were it put right—as it might be put right if people did not prefer illusions to platitudes—this world would be vastly more like heaven than it actually is, and the occupation of many futile politicians would be gone.

For if amateurishness is the world's curse (and it is), amateurishness is in a special degree the curse of the home. And let us not hide from ourselves that the home is the most important as well as the most prevalent organism in the world. It is the most important because its influence is the most constant and the most formative. Of late years the home has suffered something in the nature of a partial eclipse; it has even in some cities come to be regarded as the place which all free members of the family should avoid as far as they can. Individuals now have a habit of leaving the home in order to eat, in order to be amused, even in order to be born; they return to it in order to change their clothes, and when they are so sleepy that bed is the only resort for them. Yet in spite of its partial eclipse the home still maintains the real prominence which I have assigned to it, and its influence is still immensely greater than people generally suspect.

As for the partial eclipse, it has been due to the partial failure of the organism, which failure has without doubt been due to amateurishness. People have not rushed into the terrible promiscuity of restaurants, hotels, boarding and nursing establishments, dancing halls and places of diversion because of the high qualities of these wholesale machines in which the individual is effaced, but because they have seen in them a refuge from the shortcomings of the home. Would, for instance, any person of taste subject his idiosyncrasies and the innermost recesses of his body to the harrow of a great restaurant if he could dine to his liking at home? The great restaurant, with all its frightful faults of wholesaleness, suppression of the individual, expensiveness, and lack of delicacy, does somehow manage to beat the home in the esteem of the home-escaper. And there is no reason, save the home's amateurishness, why, except on peculiar occasions, it should beat the home. When you see a man and his wife quitting the home, and the servants and perhaps the children in the home, simply to dine at a restaurant, you may know that something is fundamentally wrong. And the business of women is to look to it.

The striking difference between other organisms and the home is that the former are characterised by professionalism and the latter is not. I do not mean that organisms directed by men are free from amateurishness. They assuredly are not. In efficiency they leave a lot to be desired (this applies damnably to organisms of government), but as a rule they do have at least an intention of professionalism; the way to professionalism is there even if it is not followed. The home does not pretend to be professionally directed; and the explanation lies in the upbringing of women, not in a sexual incapacity; for numerous elaborate and vast organisms are successfully directed by women —but women professionally trained for the job. The home alone is left to the unaided mercy of heaven.

And yet no organism demands wider knowledge and nicer skill than the home. The girl of exceptional domestic ambition or with exceptional parents learns to cook at a special educational establishment, and she is beheld as a wonder, and as being fully prepared for her task as director-general of a home. But, taking the average middle-class home, an ability to cook scarcely suffices to make a competent director-general!

The director-general ought to understand the principles of comfort. When she is buying an easy chair for the house she must be able to distinguish between an easy chair and an instrument of torture of the Spanish Inquisition. Homes have been ruined by easy chairs that were not easy, and by beds ditto. Millions of quarrels have originated in them.

Although she may not have artistic taste, she ought to understand the principles of decoration and be able to grasp the proved truth that wallpapers and curtains affect happiness and health. She ought to understand accounts, and to be versed in the ingenuities of all the kinds of tradesmen with whom she has to deal. She ought to understand the forces behind the face of a clock, and to know that if at five minutes to the hour she starts on something that will take her ten minutes the clock will show five minutes past the hour when she has done; many people go down to their graves under the illusion that the clock will show the hour—because they would like it to show the hour. She ought to understand the psychology of persons in a class different from her own, or she cannot manage her staff. She ought to be able to do everything that the staff have to do—for example, sweeping a room or carrying a loaded tray—or her moral authority over them will be impaired; nobody can successfully give instruction in a matter with which he is not practically conversant. Cookery is a case in point.

Here, then, is a fair list of essential accomplishments for the controller-general. But the catalogue is scarcely begun. The director-general should know the primary facts about the human body, male and female, and something of its pathology. Otherwise how can she keep her head and act with wisdom when some strange symptom develops in somebody and all turn to her for guidance and reassurance? She should know when to send for a doctor and when to laugh. She should understand the action of the common drugs. She should know what diets suit what conditions. She should be able to give first-aid—how humiliating to have to wring your hands and murmur soft useless words while waiting for a doctor to arrive! She should comprehend the principles of infant education. She should be full of information about hygiene. She should know how to dress and make the best of her physical self. She should be expert in conversation, and expert in utilising to the full such gifts as she possesses. Above all, she should have the art of never looking a ninny, in no matter what company.

And all these matters, with sundry others

that I have omitted, she should have studied seriously. I doubt whether there exists anywhere any school, college or university at which the full course of training for a director-general of the home can be had. I doubt whether any aspirant for the post of director-general ever thinks of acquiring ten per cent. of the proper qualifications. I am quite sure that the large majority of the aspirants do not in fact acquire five per cent. A special education extending over three years would not be too much for the business.

The marriage of Jack and Jill ought to be the conjoining of two experts. Jill's parents usually take care that Jack shall be some sort of an expert. And they almost invariably take care that Jill shall not be an expert. Too often Jill has not learnt—has not been allowed to learn—even what her parents' amateurish home could have taught her. She brings to the marital bargain a face and a heart and a pair of movable arms, and everybody assumes at first that she has thereby fulfilled her obligations. And of course she is apt to put too much faith in her contribution.

The steak is cooked to a cinder, and Jill exclaims:

"The steak is cooked to a cinder, but I am charming and I adore you."

The excuse is good enough for about twenty-five steaks, but at the twenty-sixth Jack will probably say out loud:

"Both statements are undeniable, but I fail to see the connection between them."

He may possibly go so far as to indicate that charm and adoration cannot be assimilated into masculine tissue. The bitter fruit of amateurishness is ripening, and it will have to be eaten though the steak is not.

Some may marvel that Jill does not take measures to qualify herself for the post she holds even after she has stepped into it. The omission to do so, however, is not a bit marvellous. She accepts her amateurishness as due to the secret and unalterable nature of things. And Jack does the same. Whereupon I am tempted to assert that, in that sense, the phenomenon known as "nature" simply does not exist. This is not absolutely true, but it is more true than untrue. The history of man's refusals to knuckle down to the said phenomenon is the history of human progress. Nature is terribly inefficient in the mass, and far more wasteful than the worst housewife. But the instinct to transform inefficiency into efficiency is also part of "nature," though a small part.

* * *

It may seem that my proposals for ridding women of one form of slavery may condemn them to another form of slavery, perhaps not less irksome; for whereas young men have to learn only a single business, I am suggesting that girls, hitherto consecrated to a relative indolence, should suddenly find energy to learn two! The criticism has point, and must be answered. And to answer it I would say again that, though I prophesy a new order, I do not expect it to be established and fully working the week after next. It will arrive slowly and with no more speed than the frailty of girlhood and the human nature of educational authorities permit. No charming young creature will die a martyr to my revolution.

I will take the two halves of the programme separately. The pioneers of the movement for expertness in domesticity will probably have rather a hard time. It is conceivable that their desire to take the woman's sphere quite seriously will bring down on them the traditional charge of trying to unsex themselves, to *leave* the woman's sphere. Certainly many excellent persons will hotly argue that the abolition of amateurishness in the home will involve the ruin of the home and the end of the true sweetness of family life. Resistance to such a change, however, is always part of the ecstasy of pioneering.

The real hardship will spring from the fact that educational machinery for the attainment of domestic expertness is, as I have indicated before, very much to seek, despite the deaths of many millionaires who rounded off their beautiful careers by leaving millions for the instruction of the young. The machinery will have to be enlarged and perfected; some of it will have to be created; and until this is accomplished the quest of expertness in domesticity will not be as easy as the quest of expertness in jazz-dancing. But when the first ascents of the rough road have been conquered, amateurishness will already have been left behind in the dust; the standard of efficiency in homes will have improved; and a majority, or a considerable minority, of the succeeding generation of girls will be born into a different ideal. The mothers being themselves experts, the daughters will be able to receive the first rudimentary lessons in expert domesticity at home and at an early age. Moreover, adequate educational machinery will be functioning for the final courses, and it ought to be possible for a candidate for matrimony to obtain in a year's special work the certificate without which she will be ashamed to live in the same house with her husband.

Do not in timid horror imagine that the curriculum of domestic education will be exclusively what is called "dry," and that it will not comprise those more alluring subjects which I have previously set out. The auspicious day will dawn when Girton students will study how to choose a dress and how to wear it, when it is bad form to miss the Conversation Class, and when a Chair of Coiffure makes a natural counterpart to the Chair of Comparative Philology. For none of the pre-occupations of the present western odalisque is wrong in itself; all indeed are right. The trouble is that they fill a great deal too much of the perspective.

THE ABOLITION OF SLAVERY

I come now to the other half of the programme, the affair of being able to earn a livelihood, and of actually earning one. And here we must divide girls into two classes: those who intend to adopt a professional career, ignoring the prospect of matrimony, and perhaps resolved not to allow matrimony to put an end to the career; and those who acquire the skill to earn money simply as a weapon to be used against adverse fate in the case of necessity.

It is obvious that the first class cannot and will not give the same amount of attention to domestic expertness as the second. They are on the same plane economically as men, and in expecting their meals and their slippers to be ready for them when they return home of a night, they will behave in a way not unlike men. Still, they will have a general grasp of the eternal principles of domesticity (as yet but imperfectly understood), and they will be able efficiently to superintend the competent lieutenants who are domestic on their behalf. And some branches of domesticity they will learn thoroughly, for these are essential to sound living. For example, erudition in comparative philology will be no excuse for a neglected complexion or for an inability to turn away wrath with a soft answer.

The second class will necessarily be content with a less ambitious effort in the domain of economics. These girls will follow an employment, not a career—an employment which can be dropped, and, if advisable, resumed. And—let me remark incidentally—they will not be deterred therefrom by the singular delusion (or pretext) that in so doing they are taking the bread out of somebody else's mouth. Every girl who allows herself to be supported in indolence and an exaggeration of luxury, really *is* taking the bread out of somebody's else's mouth. Whereas every girl who performs useful work for a proper wage is directly or indirectly putting bread into the mouth of everybody else in the state. But when economics are properly and widely inculcated there will be no need to insist on this elementary truth. Lastly, the second class of girls will of course, where possible, choose an employment which they can follow after or during marriage, or an employment akin to, or leading up to, such future employment.

No! You are misjudging me. I am not in the least anxious to exterminate the joy of life, nor to destroy leisure. I am an intense believer in both; and my conviction is that there will be appreciably more joy and more leisure in the time to come than there is at present.

If you ask me whether every girl without exception ought to be trained professionally either for domesticity or for an extra-domestic career, I reply that positively the only exceptions would be on the ground of ill-health or feeble-mindedness. If you ask me how I reconcile thoroughly efficient domesticity with my demand that married women should do work outside their homes, I reply that the expert domesticity of the future will be far less burdensome to the director-general than the muddling amateurishness of to-day. A professional will always do a job both better and more easily than an amateur, for the reason not only that he has greater skill, but that he can organise the job to the end of reducing effort to a minimum. Many branches of domesticity, so far as the director-general is concerned, demand knowledge rather than time, and emphatically improved housekeeping does not mean longer hours; it means shorter hours.

If you ask me whether every wife ought to have activities beyond her home, I reply: Certainly not. It is clear that in thousands of instances the domestic machine will absorb the whole of the director-general's time save that which should properly be given to leisure and diversion. I am not devising inexorable rules. The social organism of the future will be quite as elastic as ours, and probably more elastic. The era will never come when one woman (or man) is not more or less indolent than another. Some individuals are capable of nothing but indolence, and the indolence of a few of these is so delightfully done as perhaps to amount to a useful function. But the ideal of indolence, of futile costliness, will have to fade and vanish. Already the change has begun—it is perceptible. It must be quickened. What ideal will replace the departing ideal I am not rash enough to foretell.

Waste of individual force is the great stigma upon society. As more and more individuals are persuaded that even partial futility is not a virtue but a crime, society cannot fail to improve; in other words, the sum of happiness will increase. The disappearance of a "leisured class" (that is to say, a leisured sex) will not mean that more people will do the same work; it will mean that more people will do more work and more kinds of work. The amount of work necessarily left undone in the present régime is infinite. And there will always be more work than society as a whole can accomplish.

The question in the minds of most women will now be: "How is this predicted orgy of work going to react upon the exercise of feminine charm?" I am coming to that.

CHAPTER THREE: WOMEN AS CHARMERS

CHAPTER THREE

WOMEN AS CHARMERS

WOMEN constitute a spectacle, not only for man, but for mankind. When Jack takes Jill out for a walk in some public promenade he knows just as well as she knows that part of her function is to show herself, to contribute to the great spectacle of her sex. He may grumble at the cost of her clothes; he may make irrational and unfair remarks concerning the futility of mere appearances; he will almost certainly get irritable because in her anxiety about appearances she has kept him waiting at the start; nevertheless he would be discontented if she, as his own particular Jill, failed worthily to play her part in the spectacle.

The spectacle is a delight to the eye. It may, and probably does, stimulate thoughts which lead to actions that have their influence upon the future of the race; but it is primarily the eye's affair. Now there was a strange period in the history of the northern peoples when the delights of the eye were regarded with suspicion, even with disapprobation, and when it seemed to be considered that the eye was a culprit among our sensory organs and ought to be deprived of satisfaction; the other organs were entitled to their appetites, but not the eye, the theory being that "appearances" were in themselves wicked, and if they could not be suppressed should at any rate be reduced to a minimum. This period has passed away by reason of its unnatural perversity, and few regret it. The claims of the eye are now once more fully recognised.

Women are the supreme purveyors to the eye by virtue of their superior grace, beauty, and interest in line and colour; also by virtue of a fundamental quality, not to be analysed, from which these qualities perhaps spring. I do not mean that men have no spectacular value, no grace, beauty, nor interest in line and colour. They have. For no single human quality is confined to one sex; and, moreover, it is notorious that some men have more grace and beauty than some women; it is notorious, further, that women find pleasure in the spectacle of men. The broad fact, however, remains that women appeal more to the eye than men. A crowd comprising both sexes would far sooner behold a spectacle which consisted solely of women than a spectacle which consisted solely of men; and a crowd comprising only women would obtain more ocular gratification from looking at women than a crowd comprising only men would obtain from looking at men.

You may say what you please against the phenomenon that I have described. You may attribute its origin to base instincts or to fine instincts; you may assert that, in a double and derogatory sense, there is more in it than meets the eye. No matter! The phenomenon exists and it is permanent. That it has tremendous value in the world can be instantly perceived by imagining what would be the result upon our daily lives if women were never publicly seen, or if they always wore uniform, or if they had to keep to sombre colours, or if they ceased to feel an interest in costume and looks. Conceive a theatrical audience exclusively male. Conceive streets full of female dowdies and slovens. Conceive dances where the women were dressed all alike, as men are, and where they despised grace. The women might without exception be angels of goodness and acquiescence, and their invisible souls might be marvellously beautiful, but the world would be a different place and a gloomier place and a worse place, and the zest of life would be diminished. Indubitably an appreciable proportion of that which renders existence desirable depends upon the physical aspects of women in public. Part of the felicity of mankind has thus been committed to their charge. And although in giving more attention than men to complexion, costume, attitude, and movement they may be obeying an instinct, they are at the same time fulfilling a solemn social duty; they are making an essential contribution to the well-being of the body politic; and they are doing something which men cannot effectively do. And men are never jealous of their success, any more than women are jealous of the success of men in, say, feats of strength or muscular endurance.

Such is one of the great public duties of women. They also have a private duty of a similar kind. But there is this to be said against women, that whereas they are very conscientious in the first, they are often less so in the second. Their excuse must be that the private duty is more continuous and also more exacting. It is more exacting because it is both physical and moral.

As regards the physical side of woman's rôle in the home, I am not one of those who maintain that a wife must always delight the eye of her husband, and that what are called the "mysteries" of the toilet should never be performed except when he is looking the other way. The thing is impossible in any normal mode of living, and if it were possible it would be absurd and would impair a natural intimacy. But most men accustomed to women are aware that women have a tendency to general negligence when the eye of none but a husband can thereby be afflicted. I need not insist. We know what we know. The duty to the private eye is ignored when it need not be.

And wives cannot argue that husbands are similarly negligent, because men have not a similar obligation. Jill is apt to fail in the affair which she can accomplish and which Jack cannot accomplish. Jack adorns himself for dinner in precisely the same number of minutes whether the mighty of the land are coming to dine or whether he is to dine with only Jill. When Jill takes an hour and a half to adorn herself for a special occasion and two minutes for Jack alone, Jack will be thinking in his heart: "The bargain seems a bit uneven, and if I showed such apathy in keeping the wolf from the door, or in defending her against a burglar, trouble would probably ensue in this household."

And here I must refer to the delicate subject of cosmetics. I am not prepared to animadvert upon cosmetics. Indeed, I readily admit that an institution so ancient and universal must have a great deal to recommend it. Cosmetics may be unhealthy for the skin, but there are times when by deceiving the eye they unquestionably add to the joy of life. A woman seen across a theatre, however, may be quite a different apparition when separated from the observer by merely half the length of a sofa. Again I need not insist. We know what we know. It is sufficient to add that terrible revelations have occurred on sofas, that cosmetics may be admirable at one moment and repulsive at another, that cosmetics are the enemy of intimacy, and that if Jill forgets the great scientific truth that the inconvenience of cosmetics varies inversely with the square of the distance, she is behaving unfairly not only to Jack but to herself. Yet Jills exist who, lacking imagination, are guilty of this criminal folly.

I pass to the moral side, as distinguished from the physical side, of women's private duty. Men and women have many private duties in common, but just as Jill has a physical duty for which Jack was not designed by nature, so she has a corresponding moral duty. I do not wish to wear out a word which everybody understands but which nobody has successfully defined—charm. I simply mention it and point out that, besides the division of charm into physical and moral, there is a subdivision of moral charm into the charm which a woman exercises unconsciously and cannot help exercising, and the charm which she exercises consciously. It is only the last which will repay our attention. Jill has a natural gift for persuasion, for soothing, for lubrication of the wheels of existence by means of an activity which has little to do with the reasoning faculty. This gift is extraordinarily valuable. In fact it will often accomplish needful miracles when all other devices would fail.

The exercise of the gift, like the exercise of many other gifts, involves exertion and self-control. Jill usually does exercise it. But nearly all Jills, in exercising it, think that they are conferring a favour upon their Jacks and performing prodigies of self-effacement; and when they do not exercise it they argue to themselves, or even aloud: "Jack doesn't do it to me. Why should I do it to him?" The argument is not a good one. Jill in functioning as balm to an irritable Jack is no more conferring a favour upon him than he is conferring a favour upon her in earning a livelihood for her. Jack may be able to lubricate in an inferior masculine way, but the gift and the task are not specially his, whereas the gift and the task are specially Jill's. I am acquainted, and we are all acquainted, with Jills who, while doing naught but amateurishly directing the household, entirely omit the duty of moral charm. They might exercise their gift; they do not exercise it. They are cheats, for they have entered into a bargain and are not keeping it. They take more than they give. And yet if they were accused face to face of a malpractice, I expect they would be genuinely indignant.

In this connection I may cite an episode in the conjugal life of a certain contemporary Jack and Jill whom I mentioned in my first chapter. They had been married some years —more than three—and Jill had got quite accustomed to Jack, whose nightly return home no longer provided an ecstasy for her. She was also well set in the habit of owning Jack and the child. Jack especially was her property. She undoubtedly loved him much, but she had a passion for owning him rather than a passion for him. She watched him and watched over him and tended him and pruned him and pulled the dead leaves off him and watered him and turned sunshine on to him and occasionally neglected him, as if he had been a favourite plant in her garden. She would not let anybody else touch him, nor belittle him, though she could be a pretty fearless critic of him herself. She was—and still is—a nice and good woman, with plenty of charm up her sleeve, and she could be quite stylish when she chose. But she was apt to produce her charm and her *chic* by fits and starts. She would apparently forget her abilities for a period, and then she would remember them as if in a shock of awakening, and would indulge Jack and the world with great quantities of charm and *chic,* and then would forget again. In short, she was like a good many excellent wives, and just about as human as most of us.

I called in one evening. Jill was alone. She said in a casual, pleasant tone that Jack had "had to go" to his club, as if there was nothing in the least unusual about that. I at once perceived that some slight trouble had occurred between them; for it was known to me that Jack never went to his club (which was mine) at night. So I thrust Jack out of the conversation and began to talk about Jill's affairs, and in particular about a new post which she had been thinking of for herself. The Economic Circle, of which for some time she had acted as responsible housekeeping manager, had come to an end, a fate which somehow often overtakes local enterprises for the betterment of respectable and successful people's minds. The Economic Circle had started in all the bright glory of moral enthusiasm, had languished, and expired. The Lawn Tennis Club, however, continued to flourish heartily.

"I do not know that I shall take my new post at all," she said in a changed, tart tone.

I asked why.

She replied:

"*You*'ve been talking to Jack. I know you have."

You see, I was Jack's friend, and therefore she occasionally held it to be her right to regard me, in an amicable, reproachful way, as her enemy. In such crises I was privileged to receive in my person the darts which for reasons of her own she preferred not to shoot at Jack himself. I became the representative of a whole sex, which was at discord with her own sex. I saw that by chance I had stepped right into the conjugal trouble. What exactly the trouble was I never discovered, but it was connected with the proposal for her new post, to which, I may say, they had both been favourable.

"Yes," she went on, after I had murmured some fib, "Jack was very cross to-night—and, of course, he said it was my fault."

"I dare say it was," I replied.

"How do you know?" she protested. "That's just like you, that is! You don't know anything about it, and yet you say it was all my fault!"

"I didn't say that," I retorted. "What I meant was that it may very well have been your fault. Jack comes home to you. You preside over the evening. It's your show. He eats and drinks what you give him. He sits on chairs that you've appointed for him to sit on. Even the lampshades are your scheme. The whole atmosphere is yours, and you're the chief entertainer. The evening fails. Well, it's up to you. You started out to do something and you didn't do it."

"What did I start out to do?"

"Didn't you start out to make the evening pleasant for both of you. . . . He's gone to his club."

She shook her head.

"Then perhaps I was wrong," I said. "Perhaps you didn't start out to make the evening pleasant for Jack."

She answered:

"No doubt you think you're very clever."

"Not more so than usual," I protested. "But you aren't going to tell me that if you started out to charm Jack it wasn't your fault that you failed. You know as well as I do that he's nothing but a great simpleton and you can do what you like with him."

"He was cross when he came in," she said.

"He is brutal," I concurred. "But you must remember he's got responsibilites that you haven't got. Responsibilities make brutes."

"So have I got responsibilities."

"I agree fully. But you haven't got the responsibility of finding the money every month to keep this palace of yours solvent. Why should Jack provide you with food and fine raiment and servants and so on?"

She cried:

"I like that! I like that! Considering that he married me!"

"I admit he married you," I said. "But what were you doing while he was marrying you?"

"What do you mean?"

"Weren't you marrying him? If so, weren't you taking on some responsibilities? The fact is you don't deny that you have responsibilities. Indeed, you claim them. They aren't so heavy as his, but there they are. And one of them is to be a balm and not a fret-saw to Jack when he comes home cross. What have you been doing with all that celebrated charm of yours, Mrs. Jack?" My appeal to her was flattering.

She thought a moment, and then said aggrieved:

"Why should I try to charm Jack when Jack doesn't try to charm me?"

To which question I opposed another:

"Why should Jack open doors for you and raise his hat to you?"

"Because I'm a woman, of course!"

"Well," I said. "That's the answer."

She muttered gloomily and resentfully:

"That's all very well. But it's not so easy to be charming when Jack's cross and everything seems to be wrong."

"Most true!" I assented. "Most true! It is not. But you're a virtuous woman, and there's no terrific virtue in being charming when Jack's charming and everything's all right. A cat could be that! And there wouldn't be any virtue in Jack earning a living for you if sovereigns fell out of the sky. Only they don't. Jack's got a life-job. And so have you. And part of yours is to keep the savage charmed."

"Yes, and spoil him!"

"No! And not spoil him. To do it without spoiling him. To spoil him would be a crime. You have to manage to be virtuous without being criminal. History shows us, my dear Mrs. Jack, that the most powerful and successful charmers never spoiled the men they charmed."

"And yet," she said with sarcasm, suddenly sitting up straight, "both you and Jack are frightfully keen on me taking on this new post."

"What's that got to do with it?"

"It's got this to do with it," she said. "Here I am to go and work and have responsibilities same as Jack, and rush home tired out and prepare myself to charm Jack. I tell you one thing—and I know what I'm talking about—you can't be charming when you're tired out, unless you're an angel. And I'm not an angel."

"Oh, yes, you are," I contradicted her. "At any rate, you look considerably more like an angel than Jack does. But I don't want you to be an angel. Jack would hate living with an angel. An angel would drive him to his club every night of the week. And I don't want you to work like Jack does or to look at work—I mean outside work—as Jack looks at it. I entirely and absolutely admit that it would be too much to expect you to charm at full power if you were tired out. I wouldn't dream of asking you to get up before breakfast to manage your house while Jack still slept, and then go forth at the same time as Jack and toil abroad and come home two minutes before him and then miraculously meet the barbarian on the doorstep looking fresh as if you had been taken out of a drawer, and pretend that you had been waiting in idleness for him all day. No! Certainly not. Jack and this household are your chief job. All I say is that if you have more time than the job needs—and you *have,* you know—you'll do well for your soul's sake not to waste it. Wasting time is bound in the end to be bad for your charm. Using time is bound to increase it—if that's possible.

Now Jack will be back very soon. He's certain to take the last car. I'll depart. Pardon my oration."

"You've been very disagreeable," she said. "But won't you stay?"

"No," I said. "I never interfere between husband and wife."

* * *

I come now to the effect of a professional career upon feminine charm. Most men, and many women, will agree with the dictum: A woman can only think of one thing at once. The statement is, of course, exaggerated in order to emphasise the essential truth underlying it; this is a defect which it shares with all epigrams. But it is, in my opinion, a fair generalisation; though I do not mean literally that no woman can think of more than one thing at once, or that no man ever fails to think of more than one thing at once. An illustration of the truth is provided by nearly every woman who adopts a professional career. She abandons herself to the career, which becomes her religion, her god, her tyrant, her unique infatuation. She is changed into a fanatic. She will splendidly sacrifice on the altar, health, beauty, leisure, love, family ties—all. She exists for the career.

The quality is often called devotion. I do not say that it is not devotion; I do say that it is certainly due to a sexual disability to think of more than one thing at once. The result may be magnificent, but it is not life. It may be an ecstasy, but it is an ecstasy in a corridor. And it is no more a proof of self-fulfilment than the overgrown heart of an athlete is a proof of self-fulfilment. When exceptional men display the same characteristic of fanatical specialisation they grow into monsters. Some milder variant of the word ought to be invented for the description of women.

It may be said that women who have renounced all for a career and thrust the mere thought of matrimony or dalliance out of their souls do not need feminine charm. I agree, or rather I do not wholly disagree. But, in the first place, such women are in reality few; and, in the second place, their resolution (save in special circumstances) is highly reprehensible. No human being (save as aforesaid) is justified in cutting himself or herself off in thought from the other sex. To do so is to constitute oneself an enemy of the social order and to imitate the tragic eccentricity of a fakir who deliberately paralyses a limb.

The majority of professional women, however, with all their intense devotion to an idea which has no connection with sexual relations, do keep half an eye on men. The attitude of men to these women is more easy to explain than to defend. It is an attitude of mistrust. It is an attitude of jealousy. They seem to be saying to themselves: "These women can run their lives without us. These women have committed the sin of ceasing to be helpless and defenceless. They have entered our preserve, after considerable opposition which has proved futile. They have accepted our conditions. They are making good. Let us beware of them, for if we took them to wife, they would not be content to be our complement. They would have interests beyond ourselves. They might neglect us. They would assert their independence. There would be two masters by the fireside. They would argue. The *ipse dixit* of the husband would be smiled at, if not laughed at. Moreover, we detect already in their glances a certain scorn. Lastly, they have lost some if not all their charm."

Which is absurd, and numerous men, by personal experience, have proved it to be absurd. True, helplessness has charm, defencelessness has charm; particularly for the strong and the overbearing. Men are accustomed to this charm, and professional women have assuredly shed much of it. But they were thoroughly entitled to shed it, for it should belong properly only to the young. And in demanding it from modern women modern men can perhaps be convicted of an egotistical perversity somewhat akin to the perversity of the *roué* who will look at none but maids.

Modern men, on the same count, may also be charged with a reactionary timidity, and a lack of self-confidence, and a foolish desire to stop the earth from revolving. A man with a firm, scientific grasp of the fact that the earth will anyhow continue to revolve ought to welcome the idea of a challenge from an independent equal on the hearthrug. The idea ought to brace him to the fulfilment of his own possibilities, and to open up to him vistas of new thrills, excitations, and victories. He ought to perceive that he has a proud and necessary rôle to play in the education and completion of these original, daring female creatures, whose flinging of the gauntlet will sharpen his wits and waken him for the first time into really full activity.

It is admissible that professional women cannot give as much thought as the other kind to the physical cult of themselves. It is admissible, even, that out of an inverted vanity they do not give as much as they might. But, do what they will, and leave undone what they will, they cannot lose the essential charm of their sex. And, further, they possess a moral and mental equipment of experience and knowledge which infallibly adds to the range of their charm, and which, so far as it goes, renders their attractiveness as permanent as the attractiveness of men. For example, their conversion, other things being equal, must have an interesting piquancy which the non-professional woman cannot aspire to achieve. They actually have general ideas! With them, more conversational material presents itself. Conversation becomes more genuine, more honest, more invigorating, and less of a time-passing game subject to conventional rules which are irksome to both sides. And if any man says to me that he does not want this kind of conversation with his wife, I reply that either he is a highly unusual person or the truth is not in him. Most husbands sitting by their purely domestic wives in the intimate solitude of the domestic evening can remember moments when they longed for this kind of conversation with a wild, fierce longing. The disadvantage of the purely domestic woman is insipidity. It is a disadvantage whch, as the earth continues to revolve, will tend greatly to diminish.

CHAPTER FOUR: ARE MEN SUPERIOR TO WOMEN?

CHAPTER FOUR

ARE MEN SUPERIOR TO WOMEN?

TRUTH is as slippery as an eel. It never loses a chance to wriggle out of your hands. There is one truth which a man finds it difficult to hold, and more difficult to proclaim even in serious argument, in these days and in the presence of the women of these days. When I am talking to the splendiferous, peacockish women and girls who have granted to themselves all the traditional freedom of men, who have killed the chaperon and abolished the blush, and who in a social and domestic way do everything that men do (except become fathers), the truth escapes from me and I cannot recapture it. And when I am talking to the professional women and girls who have really done the work of emancipation, who have fought so tenaciously and been so roughly handled, and but for whose struggles the aforesaid female peacocks would still be cooped up in the old slavery, this truth escapes even farther from me and I dare not attempt to recapture it.

Can a decent man, and especially a man who is a convinced feminist, hold forth the horrid truth to these adventurous, valiant creatures, the one kind so brave and strutting in display, the other kind so terrifically obstinate in genuine courage? Has he the heart to do it? And if he did would he not stand a good chance of being burnt up like dry brushwood in a sudden flame of scorn?

Nevertheless one must seize and proclaim the truth again. And the truth is that intellectually and creatively man is the superior of woman, and that in the region of creative intellect there are things which men almost habitually do but which women have not done and give practically no sign of ever being able to do.

Some platitudes must now be uttered. The literature of the world can show at least fifty male poets greater than any woman poet. Indeed, the woman poets who have reached even second rank are exceedingly few—perhaps not more than half a dozen. With the possible exception of Emily Brontë no woman novelist has yet produced a novel to equal the great novels of men. (One may be enthusiastic for Jane Austen without putting *Pride and Prejudice* in the same category with *Anna Karenina* or *The Woodlanders.*) No woman at all has achieved either painting or sculpture that is better than second-rate, or music that is better than second-rate. Nor has any woman come anywhere near the top in criticism. Can anybody name a celebrated woman philosopher; or a woman who has made a first-rate scientific discovery; or a woman who has arrived at a first-rate generalisation of any sort?

The stereotyped reply to these regrettable platitudes is that only lately have women "had a chance," and that when the fruits of education and liberty have ripened women will rival men in all branches of creative and intellectual activity. Such a reply—I say it with trembling—is the reply of a partisan.

For ages women have had every opportunity that education can furnish to shine creatively in painting and in music. Thousands of women give half their lives to painting in conditions exactly similar to the conditions for males. The musical institutes are packed with women who study exactly as men study. What result in creation is visible? As for fiction, women have long specialised in it. Probably there are more women novelists than men to-day. But no modern woman-novelist has yet cut a world-figure. Innumerable women have had the leisure and the liberty and the apparatus to become philosophers, but the world has not discovered a woman-philosopher whom it could honestly place hundredth after the first ninety-nine philosophers of the other sex.

I admit that in scientific discovery, which is comparatively a new field, women ought not yet to be judged, but since the same qualities of creative imagination and intellectual power are needed here as in the other fields cited, I do not anticipate in science a greater measure of distinction for women.

In creation, in synthesis, in criticism, in pure intellect women, even the most exceptional and the most favoured, have never approached the accomplishment of men. It is not a question of a slight difference, as for example the difference between the relative proportionate sizes of the male and the female brain—it is a question of an overwhelming and constitutional difference, a difference which stupendously remains after every allowance has been made for inequality of opportunity. Therefore I am inclined to think that no amount of education and liberty of action will sensibly alter it.

But I have been comparing the greatest achievements of men with the greatest achievements of women. What about the average in each sex? The cynic—and at moments we are all cynics—might assert, after a careful survey of the intellectuality of the average man, that the intellectuality of the average woman could not possibly be lower. And, indeed, many brilliant women in their angry moods of revolt have actually said this—and may conceivably have believed it. But it is certainly contrary to broad human experience. Every man knows in his heart, and every woman knows in her heart, that the average man has more intellectual power than the average woman. It is a fact immanent in the households of the world. It is a fact as notorious as the fact that a man has more physical strength than a woman. Just as women admire physical superiority, so they admire intellectual superiority, not as a rule in the slightest degree resenting it. How often have women exclaimed with ardour: "I do *love* to listen to men arguing together"! (By some the entertainment is enjoyed like a circus.) And how is it that women gifted with an unusual allowance of intellect so persistently seek out the society of men?

Superior intellectual power means, and always did mean, domination. Women in the main love to be dominated. They are not entirely happy until they are dominated, at any rate in appearance. I feel here that I am writing like an old-fashioned man. I cannot help that. Truth is truth. I am not an old-fashioned man. I am a feminist to the point of passionateness. But at the risk of being ostracised and anathematised by all the women-feminists of my acquaintance, I shall continue to assert not only that even in this very advanced year women as a sex love to be dominated, but that for some thousands of years, if not for ever, they always will love to be dominated. This desire to be dominated is in itself a proof of intellectual inferiority. It is instinctive and it survives, despite a general impression in certain quarters that recent progressive events have in some mysterious way put an end to it.

* * *

But woman is just as human as man, and one of the major human characteristics is the wish to have one's own way. True, Jill loves to be dominated, and if Jack is not a figure sufficiently heroic for domination she will pretend to herself and others that he is more powerful than he in fact is, so that she may be dominated with decency. Nevertheless she wants to have her own way when it is opposed to his way, and she will get her own way if she can. And note that there is fun as well as credit in getting your own way against a dominating force.

It is said by the devotees of pure reason (of whom Jack is a specimen) that Jill gets her own by unscrupulous means. Not at all. Two great springs of conduct exist in the individual. One is reason; the other is sentiment. They are complementary. A world without either of them would be uninhabitable. Jack leans towards reason. Jill leans towards sentiment. Jack dominates by intellect. Jill seeks to outflank him by attacking his heart. (We are now coming as near to the root of the sex-discord as we are ever likely to come.) He may win or she may win. But, anyhow, the male domination is secretly impaired. Jack charges her with employing ruses. I agree that Jill does employ ruses, but I do not agree that she employs more ruses than Jack himself. The relations of love are full of ruses; and, in general, the keener the love the more various the ruses. Women especially may resent this statement, but who that has loved and is capable of detached observation will seriously deny it?

The matter goes deeper than the mere opposition of reason and sentiment. The evolution of human society is the result of the wavering fortunes of the endless battle between these two powers, the first of which always has ultimately won and always will ultimately win. Jack represents reason. Reason sees the advantages of change. Change means improvement. Reason is rather scornful of sentiment, and apt to be violent in the pursuit of change. Jack has initiative. And since he is also capable of defending himself and of reconstruction, he is ready to take risks. He is the progressive factor in life. But suppose that the progressive factor was unchallenged in the fulfilment of its tendency! The consequence might well be, probably would be, some kind of disaster,—a calamitous loss of equilibrium in the structure of society.

Happily, every factor in life has its counterpart. The counterpart of the progressive factor is the conservative factor. Jill sees the disadvantages of change. She knows that change may mean violence, and that violence is the enemy of beauty. She knows that change is bound to involve risk. And she hates risk because she cannot defend herself and she cannot create afresh. But she can conserve, and her function is to conserve. Moreover, being actuated chiefly by sentiment, she loves "the things that are" for their own sake. She is the sentinel of that tremendous safeguard—convention. In fine, she is the protector of man's strength against the danger due to weaknesses in it which he cannot perceive. Her rôle is therefore indispensable if the vast drama of existence is not to develop into a tragedy; and she has the qualities necessary for the rôle. Without reason, sentiment would become a quagmire. Without sentiment, reason would become an avalanche.

When each factor is an essential to life as we understand it, why argue about the superiority of one factor over the other. In this affair there are no degrees of indispensability. The indispensability is absolute in both cases. Yet people will insist upon wrangling upon that very point of relative superiority. Useless to argue to them that there is no known method of deciding whether reason is a superior faculty to sentiment, or vice versa, and that the question will never, never be decisively settled. Assuredly it is no argument to say that since reason in the end always triumphs reason must be superior to sentiment. The aim of sentiment is not ultimately to triumph but to curb and modify. Having done this, it has done what it set out to do. Quite fairly one might liken sentiment to the rider of a restless horse, the horse being reason. One might even say that sentiment is itself a kind of superior reasonableness. One might indeed invent a million ingenious propositions and images, without getting the least bit nearer to a decision.

Still, I seem to hear in the air the dissatisfied query: "You have laid it down that in at least one point man is superior to woman,—is there in your view no point in which woman is superior to man?" And the sound of the phrase "feminine intuition" seems to float towards me. I will say at once that I do not believe in woman's power of intuition. Intuition is authoritatively defined as the immediate apprehension by the mind without reasoning. If that means anything it means magic. It means something beyond commonsense and beyond explanation. Men have so-called "intuitions" perhaps quite as often as women; but they reject them, and in the long run they are justified in rejecting them. There is no husband who cannot recall the occasions when the idea contained in an intuition of his wife's had occurred to himself before his wfe uttered it; but, being a practiser of reason and perceiving that the idea was insufficiently based in reason, he had put aside the idea or reduced it to its proper place in the perspective of his thoughts.

Jack and Jill are standing in the garden and the telegraph-boy is seen approaching.

"Mother has had a stroke!" exclaims Jill.

"Nonsense!" exclaims Jack.

Now if the telegram says that one of Jack's appointments for the next day must be altered from three to three-thirty, not another word will be heard about intuition, and Jill will suffer no moral damage. Nay, she will take credit for having been wrong. But if the telegram says that Jill's mother's automobile has broken down and the old lady cannot drive over the next day, Jill will proudly cry:

"I knew it was something about mother!"

If the telegram is to the effect that Jill's mother has fallen and sprained her ankle, Jill will triumphantly cry:

"I knew something was wrong with poor mother! I had a feeling. . . ."

And the word "intuition" will supervene.

If the telegram says that Jill's mother has had a stroke, woman's claim to be an intuitionist will be firmly established in two families for about a century. Yet there will be no more in the occurrence than if Jill had backed a horse at 1,000 to 1, and the horse had won.

Intuitions are the natural resource of a type of mind which is not adept at reasoning. They are an entirely absurd substitute for reasoning. And the method of their use is unreasonable and grossly unfair, for by this method one successful intuition will far more than counter-balance a hundred failures. . . . Yes, I know that there is a thing which for convenience we call thought-transference; but I have never heard that women are more favoured than men as receptacles for transferred thoughts.

So much for feminine intuition.

However, I do believe that women are superior to men in two respects: will-power, and tenacity or perseverance. The volition of women has always struck me as terrific, compared to men's. If they can usually think of but one thing at a time, they can think of that thing with an intensity which men, upon the average, do not rival. Compared to women, men are infirm of purpose and unsteadfast,—in the working-out of an idea, in love, and beyond doubt in jealousy. Nearly all men will say that when a woman has got a notion into her head you can't get it out. But the phenomenon is nobler than that. Women in their special sphere are magnificent as preservers; they are sublime. Among all social classes ordinary women, by the most implacable volition and the most astounding eternal devotion to an idea, have preserved healths, lives and homes when the task was so formidable and apparently hopeless that not one man in ten thousand would have persisted in it. And this fact is well known. It is within the experience of everybody.

Some may ask how the mighty outburst of feminism which has marked the last decade or so squares with the theory of women as conservatives which I, following greater authorities, have put forward. The answer is that it does not. It does, however, square with the larger and more important theory that women are human. Many, if not most, men have a loose notion at the back of their minds that women ought to be something other than human, ought to be dehumanised specialists in acquiescence. That women, like men, are specialists in the scheme of things is certain. But in the first place they are not specialists in acquiescence; and in the second place they are human in the same way as men are human, before they are specialists. This truth is obvious, yet we are apt to lose sight of it.

The nineteenth century was a tremendous period of evolution. I should not be disposed to deny that it saw more evolution than any other century within historical record. Inevitably women felt the disturbance caused by the vast social movements. And towards the close of the century they began to notice that evolution had not done quite as much for them as clearly it ought to have done. In other words, freedom had not kept pace with knowledge. They felt as though men had discovered some strange new exciting spectacle. They had been imprisoned for ages, and prison had seemed natural. Now prison seemed unnatural.

Women opened their eyes and said:

"We have heard of prisons. But, by Juno! we are *in* one. We must get out. We will get out. After all we are human beings, and human beings have rights."

A sense of injustice grew in them more

and more rapidly. The leaders of them were obsessed, not inexcusably, by one idea. Specialism did not entirely cease, but to a certain degree it fell into abeyance. Human beings inspired by a sense of injustice have less time and less inclination than usual to be specialists. And the only specialism which flourishes in an insurrection is the specialism of violence.

Further, in the whole business women were merely copying men, taking advantage of the experience of men. They were not creating. They were not striking out a new path. The trail was well blazed for them. In following it they probably showed more devotion than men have shown; and no doubt their behaviour was characterised by that simplicity and unity of aim which as a rule does characterise the actions of women. No doubt it also exhibited that faultiness of perspective which makes women relatively so dangerous when they happen to inaugurate a crusade. How the crusade might have developed had the war not supervened no man can tell, but it could only have had one end, for, if the affair was a struggle between sexes, the male sex was fatally handicapped by the fact that numbers of the most intelligent men had gone over to the enemy. Indeed, the opponents of the crusade contained a huge majority of the unintelligent. Thanks to the war, the end of the crusade came with dignity. No sooner did women start to assume a specialist rôle in the war than everybody realised that the crusade had been successful. Feminism in its more stormy aspects may at one time have borne some resemblance to what is at present called Bolshevism. In reality it never had the slightest genuine tinge of Bolshevism. I have named it a crusade, and a crusade it was. But essentially women were never more feminine than when crusading. Some of them admittedly shed some feminine qualities, but merely so that other feminine qualities might have wider scope. And throughout their humanness was intense.

* * *

The feminine pendulum will swing too far. Pendulums always do. (That is why clocks go.) As I have before indicated, it is already dangerous in certain circles to doubt whether anything that is possible to men is impossible to women—anything, I mean, that in the opinion of those circles is worth doing. Such a mental attitude is bound to end in disillusion. There are certain changes which no amount of education, opportunity, and experience can bring about. You might educate generations of men for centuries to manage a *crêche;* they might acquit themselves creditably in the task; they might even do some parts of it better than a mother who trusted solely to the promptings of the maternal instinct. But they would never do it half as well as women who had had only a twentieth of their education. They would always have the air of trained animals; and I question if they could possibly escape being ridiculous. Education will bring out; it cannot put in. Education will enable women to avail themselves of new opportunities until recently denied to them. And experience, the slow growth of custom, and above all the changed attitude of the world towards them will enable them to act generally in fresh rôles with an assurance and decision of touch not yet attained.

But just as no training will change the primary sexual faculties, so no training will change the secondary sexual faculties. Even the minor sexual faculties cannot be tossed to and fro from sex to sex. Woman is rational (though I have heard the assertion contradicted), and man is sentimental. Nevertheless, in the average woman reason will never assume the throne of sentiment. Education and opportunity will improve the rational quality in woman; but they will also improve the sentimental quality. The proportions will not alter. They cannot. Why should they? The sequel will inevitably be that woman, having advanced, will be precisely woman. That is the point to which every avenue leads. But before the sequel is reached there will in all likelihood be some rough going.

One thing is sure—that women will have a much better time in the future than they have had in the past. I do not mean that they will necessarily be happier. My theory is that happiness is stationary over long periods, as artistic excellence is stationary. I mean that they will fulfil themselves more completely. To die feeling that you have really lived is better than to die happy. But fulfil themselves as much as they may, women will never get beyond the function of being the complement of men. And lest I may be misunderstood, let me add that men will never get beyond the function of being the complement of women.

It is an advantage of men that they show no desire to be women. Women, intoxicated with newly revealed possibilities, have had a tendency to imagine that nature has forbidden naught to them. The tendency in the circumstances is excusable by men. But nature does not accept excuses, and the vagaries due to the tendency will have to be redeemed in suffering. No new sex is going to be created. The ancient frontiers will continue. Women used to be kept far away from the frontier. They can now march right up to it—and look over—but they will not step over. Men do not expect women to be everything, and similarly women cannot expect to be everything. The sex which produced Sappho, Saint Teresa, Ninon de l'Enclos, Louise de la Vallière, Florence Nightingale, Jane Addams, did so by virtue of profound characteristics which will for ever be predominant in the sex. The converse of the statement is self-evident.

With all this, I should like to offer a gleam of hope to those ardent feminine souls who resent, and always would resent, the "domination" of men, even if the domination is more spectacular than effective. The human mind can conceive a period—not the day after to-morrow!—when the organisation of society will be so immensely improved that in no matter what climate the satisfaction of all physical needs, including the most refined and elaborate, will have become a mere bagatelle in the sum of social activity; a period when no individual will have to worry for more than ten minutes a day about things like food, clothing, and shelter, and when no individual will be forced to soil his hands in order to exist. A period, too, when the perfecting of mechanical resources will have rendered sexual differences in muscular strength of no account whatever. Such a period may well be a period of cautious conservation preparatory to some new outbreak of mental activity beyond our present imagining. It may well be a period of melancholy and disillusion, when the violent male spirit of experimental adventure would be held to be a danger to the marvellous fabric of human relations. In such a period the general sense of mankind would probably accord the leading rôle to women, to the sex of conservers, the sex which holds fast to that which is and refuses to be tempted into the perils of the untried and the unknown. Women would then, in the jargon of that day, have risen to be the "superior" sex, because reason would be under a cloud and sentiment the sole anchor of safety. The foregoing is a vision, and at best whole civilisations will have risen and decayed ere anything resembling it is realised. Still, it may console.

CHAPTER FIVE: SALARY-EARNING GIRLS

CHAPTER FIVE

SALARY-EARNING GIRLS

YOUNG girls have always been held to be very mysterious. To-day they are held to be more mysterious than ever. Such at any rate is the view taken by people of middle-age, both men and women, and their attitude to the "typical" young girl has in it a certain amount of reproach. But whether young men regard their feminine contemporaries as specially mysterious I doubt. And the young are the best judges of the young. (Though old, I assert it.)

Before going further, let me interject that when I say "young girl" I mean what the French mean when they say *jeune fille*—that is, an unmarried adult virgin who is not old enough to be called a spinster. I will not attempt to determine at what age an unmarried virgin begins to incur the terrible imputation of spinsterhood; it varies, being dependent on a lot of things, such as colour of hair, litheness of frame, complexion, ankles, chin (the under part), style of talk and of glance. I have known spinsters of twenty-five, and young girls of at least forty. Henceforward in this chapter I intend to discuss that very large middle class of girls whose members wholly or partly earn their own living. Unfortunately this class does not yet by a long way comprise all girls; nevertheless, its demeanour towards life influences and explains the demeanour towards life of the "leisured class" of girls above it, and therefore in some degree it is representative of that class also.

The root of modern feminism is, of course, the desire for money—money that can be transformed into personal satisfactions. True, the pioneers of feminism did not think primarily of money when they set out on those adventurous careers which too often involved obloquy and even martyrdom. They thought primarily of freedom—freedom to fulfil themselves according to their individual instincts. But freedom includes, and must include, economic freedom; and economic freedom signifies the control of the means of living.

How many pioneers would, for example, have given up the fight against the medical societies for the right to practise as doctors if the medical societies had said to them: "You may practise as doctors, but you must not charge fees"? None. The right to earn, to be economically free, was the essence of the struggle.

After the pioneers had turned the tide of the battle, and cleared many paths for the multitude, the multitude began to follow from no other motive than an economic motive. The mass of girls saw a chance of obtaining for themselves a share of that strange and delectable commodity, money, and they took it. If they did not take it of their own accord their parents little by little insisted on their taking it, and finally, in the middle-class under review, the general rule was established that girls must earn. A few of them go out into the world against their will. On the other hand, a few would have gone out even if no money had resulted from the process, simply to escape an oppressive atmosphere at home, and to breathe the fresh winds of the world. But the great mass, the all-but totality, go out solely in search of money and the economic freedom which money confers on its possessors.

The consequences were not entirely advantageous. The girls lost the old girlish air of ignorance, of being simpletons in the world. But that was an advantage. They lost the attractiveness of perfect inexperience. That, too, was an advantage, for such attractiveness appealed chiefly to the perverse and the oriental in the male sex. They lost much futile leisure; that too was an advantage. They lost some of their ideals, and that, though not an unrelieved disadvantage, was a disadvantage. They lost, thousands of them, a measure of health; for, being raw and eager, they were, and still are, often exploited in the conditions of employment, overworked, and sweated. That was an unrelieved disadvantage, and all the more so because it filled them with a sense of resentment against the men who exploited them and against the innocent men who received (and still receive) more pay than they for precisely the same work.

But the gain on the whole was enormous. There was, at first, the novel and dignifying sensation of the performance of a useful function in society. Certainly the mere novelty of the sensation soon departed, and girls of the present and the future do not, and probably will not, recapture it. But the sensation itself remains, though it is chiefly subconscious, and though it may be mingled with the quite different sensation of the oppressiveness of work. People, even enthusiastic girls, as a rule start the week's work with the complaint uttered or unexpressed: "Monday morning again! What a grind!" They do not arise on Monday morning with hearts full of heavenly gratitude for the privilege of being allowed to perform a useful function in society. Still, the gratitude vaguely persists and it gives birth to pleasurable pride.

Then, there is the advantage of meeting men other than near relatives. Under the old régime, middle-class and also lower-middle-class girls met men in a sort of ceremonial—except sometimes when they met them by ingenious and conspiratorial design. They elaborately prepared themselves for meeting men. Before meeting men they pondered long over the encounter, and after meeting men they pondered long over the encounter. Under the new régime girls who work meet as many men in a day as their predecessors of similar standing met in a month. Indeed, many of their predecessors met men (other than relatives) about as often as they met giraffes. It is, I admit, a fact that girls who work, particularly those whose work is clerical, are now during working hours confined more and more to the companionship of girls. Frequently in large establishments they find girls on either side of them, in front of them and behind them; they are supervised by girls and they have girls under them. And they might be excused for thinking that they had fallen into a nunnery instead of into a factory or an office. But those vast interiors are not after all nunneries. The male is there and the influence of the male is there; and, further, the morning and evening promiscuity of the public vehicle has to be brought into account.

Save in highly exceptional instances, the girl who earns her living abroad acquires in doing so one of the most important and healthy experiences of feminine life—familiarity with the masculine. She is bound to be constantly correcting her dreams of men by the reality of men. And the correction, stretching over a considerable period, is less violent and distressing than it would be if concentrated into, say, a month of marriage.

Lastly, the salary-earning girl gains knowledge of the world. This knowledge may be superficial, imperfect, one-sided, mischievous in certain respects, but it is far better than ignorance. She does get some sort of a notion of the structure and working of society; she does get some sort of a notion of real values: which notions, even if they be pitifully vague, do enable her on frequent occasions to reject the dangerous poison of sentimentality which would otherwise be poured into her by the older persons whose object in life seems to be to confuse that which ought to be with that which is. To anybody who demands sceptically: "But after all can the girl teach her grandmother to suck eggs?" I would reply: "As a rule, she can."

How does she gain this knowledge of the world? It would be more reasonable to ask how she could avoid gaining it. All day the world is rubbing off information on to her. Even if she sits with a thousand girl-colleagues in some clacking interior of a Chicago mail-order house and does nothing for eight hours but tap out bills on a typewriter, she is learning about the kind of things that people really do want and how much they want them, and what wild sums they are ready to pay for them. She cannot travel with regularity through a city on the top of a 'bus, or under a city in a tube, without effectively learning more about the world than she would learn from a hundred books and a hundred parents in a hundred years.

She reads the newspaper. It teaches her. She may read it simply for distraction on the daily journey. It teaches her. It may teach her badly. It teaches her. She may not read a newspaper, but only look at the pictures in a newspaper. The pictures teach her. I would sooner that she read the newspaper than any of the vast majority of novels. If she reads the latest old-fashioned sweet novels she is severely handicapped, for the latest old-fashioned novelists are still catering for the girl's grandmother, and the perusal of one of them may almost undo in half an hour's train journey at night all the solid educational work that contact with the world has accomplished in ten hours.

Then she visits restaurants, either public

or private—not places where there is a conspiracy of waiters to convince her that she is a most high queen surrounded by slaves; but hurrying, realistic places where the principles which rule the world stand forth naked, and everybody not merely knows, but openly admits, what is what; and she will not obtain value for her money in such places until she has genuinely obtained a grasp of the aforesaid principles.

And when she reaches home and sits down to the family meal she finds that the conversation is much more instructive, candid, catholic, and interesting than it used to be before she went into the world. The most arrogantly male father, the most head-burying ostrich of a mother, cannot decently pretend that exactly the same girl has come home who went forth. And the conversation improves accordingly.

All that I have just written is obvious, and perhaps I ought to apologise for having put it under the gaze of the enlightened reader. Nevertheless, I observe on every hand men and women old enough to know better who seem to be struck into astonishment by the obviously inevitable consequences of these obvious facts. A grey-haired lady, who had travelled much and could look after herself very well, said to me yesterday: "The modern girl (meaning the girl who earns a living) is a complete mystery to me. I cannot understand her. She is so mature. She has opinions about everything. She is ready to talk about everything. She is so sure of herself."

Here are four assertions about the modern salary-earning girl.

First, she is so mature. Well, she has to seem mature in order to get a livelihood. When the grey-haired lady was young it was her business, and the correct thing, to seem immature and naïve. In both cases there was exaggeration, but the modern example really is more mature than her forerunner, though not so mature as she would like to appear.

Second and third, she has opinions about everything and is ready to talk about everything. Well, unless she was sent out into the world with a chaperon and persuaded not to read newspapers, and was gagged and rendered deaf by wax in her ears, and was forbidden to cerebrate, she could not help having opinions about everything and talking about everything. You cannot, under pain of being taken for a lunatic, say to a girl whom you push forth alone into the world and who has eyes to read a newspaper: "You must pretend that the world does not exist and that beyond the garden wall there is naught but void."

Fourth, she is so sure of herself. Well, she isn't. She is only pretending to be sure of herself. Like nearly all the young people that ever lived she has a desire to be taken seriously on the matters which interest her, and her apparent self-confidence is a bid for serious attention. The grey-haired lady was just the same, but on more restricted matters, when she herself was young. Nothing is easier, and few things are more cruel, than for a really experienced and knowledgeable older person to put his adult foot through the thin crust of a girl's cocksureness.

But the grey-haired lady had a fifth indictment of "the modern girl." The modern girl is so fond of pleasure! If the middle-aged were to say: "The modern girl is so fond of work," I could see the point of the remark. For the outstanding thing about the modern girl is that she is fond of work.

Admitted, she is fond of pleasure. All young people are fond of pleasure, and if they are not then there is something wrong with them. The grey-haired lady when her hair was golden was precisely like the modern girl in this: she took all the pleasure that the social machine offered to her. Often it was little enough, perhaps. To my mind the tragedy of existence—provincial existence in particular—fifty years ago lay in the failure of communities to organise themselves for pleasure. The doom of ennui lay upon whole districts, including the suburbs of great capitals. And it was terrible and its effects were vicious. That is altered, and is being still further altered. Society has organised itself better for work, and better also for pleasure. Life is made to yield more than it used to yield, and yet life lasts longer and youth lasts longer.

The modern girl seizes her opportunities, —she does no more. The increase of opportunity is due to the improvements in education—and in transport. It is due, that is to say, to improved work, part of which work is done by the modern girl herself. And since work precedes pleasure, and the energy of the modern girl is finite, she is very unlikely to carry pleasure to excess. If she did, it would as usual cease to be pleasure.

Much is said about the modern girl's craze for dancing. But seeing that the modern girl dances with the modern youth the alleged craze cannot be charged against one sex only. And is it necessary to point out that dancing is not an invention of the present age? On the contrary, the erudite affirm that dancing is among the oldest, if it is not the oldest, of human diversions. No later device has surpassed it in healthiness, sanity and pleasure-giving quality. Probably there never was a time when healthy girls were not "crazy" for dancing. If the modern girl dances more than her ancestress, the explanation is that nowadays a dance can be arranged and carried out with less than a tenth of the trouble necessary in the past, and that communities have discovered their own vast potentialities for organised enjoyment. The explanation is certainly not that something sinister and incomprehensible has happened to the modern girl.

* * *

I began by expressing a doubt as to whether the modern young man looks upon the modern girl as mysterious. We may now dismiss the doubt. He does not. Nor does he regard her as sinister. At any rate, he does not regard her as more sinister or mysterious than his father regarded his mother. It may be taken as absolutely certain that he regards her as quite the usual and proper thing, and that she has the same view of herself. There are probably several millions of her in Britain, and more millions of her in America. If she could by some magic be transformed into such a girl as the grey-haired lady would deem ordinary and comprehensible, the young man would pass by on the other side of the street in alarm or disdain when he saw her approaching. And if by chance he was caught in the net of the companionship of the changed girl, he might be excused for imagining that he had encountered a woman out of the East, a creature slipped forth from behind the purdah.

He would say to himself:

"How queer this girl is! She doesn't know anything about anything. You can't talk to her about trains, tubes, motor-bus routes, season-tickets, typewriters, tea-shops, cigarettes, music-halls, offices, subscription dances, filing systems, hours of work, bridge, actresses, politicians, politics, strikes, income tax, housing problems, excursions, motor-bikes, football, newspapers, law cases. In fact, there's nowhere to begin, and she needs looking after like a baby in a perambulator. Where on earth was she brought up? Has she just come to life, or has she just been taken out of a cupboard and unwrapped?"

He would conclude that despite a queer charm which emanated from her, she was artificial, even perverse, and above all he would conclude that she lacked savour—curtly, that she was dull. He would murmur that he really didn't know what girls were coming to, and his attitude would be a justifiable attitude. It is the attitude of the grey-haired lady, and of all us middle-aged and aged, that cannot be justified. We are continually afraid that some section of humanity (not our own section, of course) has forsaken nature. I would not assert that no large section of humanity ever swerves into the unnatural. Instances might be found in history of a large section having done so under the stress of some mighty calamity. But such swervings are never gradual; they are sudden; and I question if they have ever been limited to one sex. The present change in girls has been gradual; it is entirely explicable; and it is a change from the less natural to the more natural. So the costumes painted by Velasquez were less natural than crinolines, and crinolines less natural than the most eccentric frocks of to-day.

The present change in girls signifies a *rapprochement,* a fraternisation, of the sexes. The modern girl, startling though she is to the grey-haired lady, behaves more in accordance with human instincts than the grey-haired lady ever did in girlhood; and she has quite as much real dignity. Indeed, it may be argued that she has more real dignity. She can meet the male companion in a hundred matters on common ground. Their mutual interests are not confined to passion and pleasure, but stretch over about two-thirds of life. Their intercourse is freer, fuller, saner, more amusing, more serious, and less perverse. That all is perfect in their relationships, and the millenium already arrived upon us, I do not feel utterly convinced; but I do anticipate with satisfaction the time when the modern girl will be more plentiful than she is. A huge number of ancient girls are still being educated among us. The grey-haired lady smiles upon these latter as normal, as "real girls," as the only "nice" girls. But they are not normal. They are an anachronism, and they will vanish. They are vanishing.

Of course, the salary-earning girl is that terrible thing, a money-grubber. She wants money, either for herself or for others, but usually for herself, and she plunges into the ignoble world in order to get it. Money always costs a price. She pays the price in the loss of qualities of ignorance and naïveté and dependence which once were highly esteemed; and she pays it in hard work, often in discomfort, and sometimes in impaired health. Money is partial or complete economic freedom, which is what she is after. Not long ago no right-thinking girl would have dared to think practically about economic freedom. It was the last attribute that a man desired a girl to possess. And if by some freak of inheritance a girl did possess it, the man who made her his wife generally took steps, the law aiding him, to dispossess her.

Even to-day there are women, mothers of families, who cannot leave the house and take a taxi without previously asking for the money for the mad adventure, because they are never allowed the uncontrolled use of any money at all. These women are survivals from the grand romantic past, the past of which too many of us regret the disappearance. And if in their youth they had set about the business of acquiring economic freedom, their guardians would have treated them as if they had set about to become dancers in a sailors' café. Romance, as is well known, has died. Notions like economic freedom have killed it. Could an age in which maidens soil themselves by worldly contacts for mere money and economic freedom be other than unromantic? Impossible! The great complaint of the aged woman against the young is that the young are so "painfully" unromantic and matter-of-fact.

The brazen creatures actually face facts; they actually hate to be dependent idlers and ninnies—that is to say, to be in economic slavery. And so they—more than men, it seems—have committed the murder of romance.

But romance is not quite dead after all. Indeed, it is probably more alive than ever; for, curiously enough, as knowledge increases, so does the sense of romance and wonder. The modern girl, when she steps into the world, takes all her girlishness with her. Numerous observers have attested that she took it all with her when she put on khaki and transported herself to the fields of war. And in peace she trails it along all the corridors of all the offices and manufactories and ministries. In a word, love-making, which is the foundation stone of romance, persists. The aged woman aforesaid will say that it persists too lustily. But what the excellent dame means is that love is not now made precisely in the same manner as when *she* inspired young men to buy flowers and to hang around.

And we must indeed admit that grave changes have occurred since all brides were either stolen or bought, and since a bride who was neither stolen nor bought suffered on that account some loss of prestige and public respect. Nowadays when a young man makes love he cannot talk through his hat quite as much as his ancestor of five thousand years ago, or even of fifty years ago. In the salary-earning girl he meets somebody who is nearly his equal in material matters, and his remarks to her are likely to be tested at every point by experience—experience of men, experience of economics, experience of life.

Is, then, love reduced to prose? Not in the slightest degree. There is less bargaining than ever there was, and such bargaining as remains is much less crude and much less one-sided than the old bargaining. Love has a larger scope than aforetime, and the temptations to ignore love and to pretend that love exists when it does not are immensely fewer. . . . So that money-grubbing is thus demonstrably not an unmitigated evil. We may go further and say that, practised in moderation, it is an unmitigated good and the parent of happiness, justice and sound sagacity.

Girls marry later than they used to marry; therefore men also. I have heard expressions of wonder that economically independent girls should marry, not later, but at all. This wonder is, of course, misplaced. The modern girl marries because, though her position as a maid is much more advantageous than that of her forerunner, she still has a lot to gain by marriage. She still has more to gain by marriage than a man has to gain, and herein is the main reason why the male sex is to this day the sought-after sex. She is not creative; she is not fully capable of self-defence; she does not shine in initiative; she is less complete in herself than a bachelor in himself; she is very human in that she does not love work for work's sake; she would like a change; she has dreams, hopes; she is afraid of the reproach, half pitying, half disdainful, which society still puts upon the maid who passes a certain age without capturing a man; she longs for the unique feminine dignity of wifehood and motherhood and home-mistress-ship; she is not averse from ruling a man and a family.

None of these considerations is the chief

consideration in consenting or plotting to marry: but every one of them pushes the girl on. The chief consideration is that she naturally, profoundly, and rightly wants Man, just as an individual man wants Woman; and this instinct is almost bound, rather sooner than later, to narrow itself to a powerful inclination for an individual man. The motive to marry is not so urgent with her as it was with her predecessor; but, on the other hand, the inclination is likely to be more powerful, because, meeting more men and being a better judge of men, she stands a better chance than her forerunner of meeting just the man calculated by nature to arouse the inclination in precisely her. Once the inclination is set up and the instinct actuated, most if not all economic arguments will dissolve before it. Desirable as economic independence may be, the great truth is revealed that there are things even more desirable. Moreover, marriage for her does not invariably involve the loss of economic independence. In the majority of cases it does, but not in all. And when it does, and she cheerfully doesn't mind, we see that the mighty course of evolution is not sensibly deflected by those social phenomena of change which inspire the timid among us with a foolish fear that the world is coming to an end.

CHAPTER SIX: WIVES, MONEY AND LOST YOUTH

CHAPTER SIX

WIVES, MONEY AND LOST YOUTH

THE great modern analysts of the sexual relationships—Balzac, Stendhal and Paul Bourget—seldom or never, I think, seriously " descended " to economics. Balzac was an all-round realist, and the " Human Comedy " is full of money; but his treatises on marriage are in the main characterised by superficial flippancy and cynicism. Bourget is generally too elegant, finicking and snobbish to mention money. Stendhal, while profoundly and magnificently romantic, did not perceive the romance of economics. My notions about girls are built on economics, doubtless to the disgust of the sentimental, who will assert that I have no soul, that I am prosaic, that I am a gross materialist, that I am blind to romance, and even that I am the murderer of romance. Still, there it is! And as my thoughts concerning the state of girls run basely to economics, so do my thoughts concerning married women. I cannot escape from it because my constant preoccupation is freedom, and, as I have said before, freedom cannot be real unless it comprises a measure of economic freedom. This is true not merely of our alleged materialistic age, but of all ages. It is no more true now than it was a thousand years ago.

The sentimental object: "What matters in marriage is not money, but affection." True, affection matters supremely in marriage—especially after the first few years, when passion has expired—but no amount of affection, whether one-sided or mutual, will turn slavery into freedom. Affection may soften the bonds; it will not loose them; and the effect of them will remain as a permanent factor in the equation that we call matrimony. Everything that enters into the composition of the relationship makes a difference. In things social, as in science, nothing disappears, nothing is negative; each element counts. And if the economic slave cries ecstatically: "I am happy," you have only to penetrate far enough into the intimacy of her heart in order to learn that what she means is: "*In spite of all* I am happy." Which, being interpreted, signifies: "I am unhappy too, but my happiness exceeds my unhappiness."

Do I seriously lay it down that the married woman of to-day is economically a slave? I do, in the majority of cases. And I add that this condition of hers colours the whole of marriage for her.

Ask the young woman who gives up a salaried situation for a husband whether she does not feel the shackles.

Watch the demeanour of the married woman who has money of her own which her husband cannot touch or will not touch. Watch the demeanour of the married woman who has no money of her own but who has had force enough to obtain control of her husband's money. Compare the demeanour of these women with the demeanour of the majority of married women, and you will (I hope) admit the immense influence of economics in the entire field of matrimony. The two demeanours are so different—sometimes subtly, sometimes spectacularly—that almost at first sight you can say with confidence: "That woman controls money," or "That woman is an economic slave." And the bright beams of conjugal affection will not suffice to blind your judgment. The partial abolition of the laws which once enabled the husband to say to his wife, "What's yours is mine, and what's mine's my own," has had the incidental advantage of letting us see plainly the difference between slavery and freedom for a woman; for in former times marriage meant economic slavery for all women, even the women who brought vast property into the connubial bargain.

The good husband, the generous husband, who has read me so far protests here:

"But my wife has an ample allowance."

Exactly. And you, my fine fellow, are regarded as good and generous because you do an act of bare justice—because you are not guilty of an obvious injustice. You even regard yourself as good and generous on this account. The day has not yet dawned when society is not somewhat startled and pleased by the sight of a husband who in economics actually plays fair! Magnanimous husband! His noble nature forbids him to take advantage of his position. There still lingers among us the odd theory that a married woman who is put into possession of money ought to be thankful, that somehow she is not really entitled to the possession of money.

And, good and generous husband, I beg to direct your attention to that word which you have employed: "Allowance." The whole situation is implicit in that word. You "allow." You permit. You vouchsafe. You needn't; but you do. You have the right to withdraw what you grant. The thing is compassionate. You might think better of it. So the recipient had better be careful, lucky creature! Indeed, the word demands serious examination. We will, however, pass the word and come to the fact.

Many husbands will say: "My wife has the spending of more money than I spend myself." It may be true; it often is true. The housekeeping allowance may well easily exceed the husband's expenditure. But, as to the housekeeping allowance, the wife is only the husband's agent. She is an agent—though perhaps with a little more liberty to exercise initiative—as the husband's cashier at the office is agent for the petty cash. She allots the money as she chooses (provided she can suit the husband's appetite), but she is obliged to spend it on housekeeping. If she "saves on" the housekeeping and makes no secret of her economy, the chances are a hundred to one that the husband will reward her by saying: "You can manage with less." Hence it is that multitudinous wives do make a secret of their economies in housekeeping and enter upon careers of deceit. Trifling deceit. Excusable deceit. Justifiable deceit. But deceit! Involving what we term the "double life." Who has not heard the wife say, with an archness that covers uneasiness and humiliation: "I don't tell my husband, naturally."

The wife usually, though by no means always, is "allowed" other money for dress. In England the wife's dress "allowance" is on the average too small; often it is absurdly small, and the wife is therefore constantly engaged in the performance of miracles, and in proving, to the confusion of science, that something can be created out of nothing. But even in the rare instances in which the dress "allowance" is adequate, it is definitely an allowance for dress; and once more the lady finds herself without genuine financial control. She spends, but the nature of her spending is fixed in advance.

Beyond the two aforesaid "allowances," ninety per cent. of wives whose husbands are in an affluent or comfortable position get naught—unless they ask for it. And when they ask they have to submit to cross-examination, perhaps criticism, perhaps protests, perhaps refusal. And at best they have to submit to receiving a favour. Necessarily they are continually aware of the sensation of being liable to render an account of their acts. They have no financial margin for whims, secrecies, foolishness, wastefulness. Contrast the case of the husband. It occurs, of course, in many families that there is no financial margin anywhere. But if there is one the husband monopolises it. He knows the proceedings of his wife; she does not know his proceedings. Husbands exist and flourish who, living on a salary, omit to tell their wives the amount thereof, or understate it. When a husband behaves foolishly in a financial sense he is not distressed by the idea that his wife will complain; his wife won't know anything about it.

His wife will never say to him: "Look here, you had two pounds loose in your pocket yesterday, and there's only two shillings to-day. How extravagant you are! Do you think we are made of money!"

The husband is not liable to render an account. He conducts his operations in the dark, secure from inquisition and judgment. And I doubt whether there is anything on earth which the average husband cherishes more than this darkness and this security from family interference and critical curiosity.

I admit that not every husband falls within my description. I know of husbands who disclose all to their wives, who treat their wives absolutely as equals in the region of finance, and allot to them the same freedom as they allot to themselves. I know of husbands who owe their financial stability to the wisdom of wives, and who do not deny it. I know of husbands who, so far as means go, never say "No" to their wives and never display an inquisitiveness such as they themselves would resent. I know of husbands who, while earning all the family money, have sunk to be the slaves of their wives in regard to the disposition of the money. But I consider that I have fairly described the average case. And if I were to emphasise the exceptions on one side, I should have to emphasise the exceptions on the other. For I should have to tell about the husbands with a mania for keeping their wives in total ignorance of the financial position, or for deliberately deceiving them concerning it; and about the wives, mentioned in a previous chapter, who are never allowed the handling of any cash at all (though possibly given permission to shop on credit to an extent almost unlimited); and about the ageing wives who see their own daughters in possession of a financial freedom which is denied to their grey hairs. And I should have to discuss the influence of such extraordinary conditions upon the sexual relation. And the digression would be still less agreeable than my main theme dealing with the average.

When all is said for and against the wife and for and against the husband in this complicated and delicate affair, it will not be denied that the average wife has a substantial grievance, or that the injustice from which she suffers must diminish the sum of her happiness in matrimony, besides encouraging her to courses of conduct which are manifestly bad for character. The average wife is in one exceedingly important respect at the mercy of another human being—her husband. This ought not to be. She has done nothing to merit her servitude. She has committed no dreadful sin which should debar her from the exercise of the common rights of an adult individual. The fact that by mutual arrangement she undertakes duties—some of them may not be easily definable, but they are there—which are not paid for in cash cannot fairly disentitle her to the undisputed control of cash. She should be so situated as to be able to gratify whims of her own instead of being exposed for ever to the whims of another.

The evolution of ideas has now passed the stage at which, economically, women lived on sufferance and the general conscience was not outraged thereby. The organisation of the social system has, as usual, lagged behind the march of ideas: but we have scarcely yet noticed the discrepancy. We are apparently incapable of being greatly shocked by what is. Thus we see two sisters, A and

B, who go out into the world. A takes employment in business and has almost precisely the freedom of a man. She may not have much money, but with what she has she does as she likes. She is at liberty to fulfil herself, whether in common sense or in foolishness. B takes to marriage. She probably works just as hard as A. She has no less responsibility. She is quite as useful to the world. Her function in the social organism has quite as much prestige. . . . Nevertheless, compared to A she is at an immense economic disadvantage; for she is obliged to explain, to justify, to entreat, to cajole, or to deceive in order to do things which A never thinks twice about. A is economically free. B is economically a slave. We see this very strange phenomenon, I say, and are not shocked. It seems to us entirely natural that a married woman should be penalised, and our first impulse, on the anomaly being pointed out to us, is to invent ingenious arguments which demonstrate that everything is all right after all, and that the married woman is not penalised, and that if she is penalised she prefers to be penalised and it is the will of Heaven that she should be penalised and to attempt to lift the penalty would be sacrilege. I need not trouble with those ingenious arguments; they are rather like the ingenious arguments which scarcely a hundred years ago respectable people brought forward to show that the penalty of death ought not be lifted from sheep-stealing and the penalty of transportation for life from orchard thefts; they are like all arguments in favour of the *status quo* merely because it is the *status quo*. I will ignore those arguments and dogmatically assert that something ought to be done about the economic slavery of the average married woman.

Oh! The reform is not easy. And certainly it cannot be simple. I am not going to propose anything revolutionary; for, first, it would never gain acceptance, and, second, if it did it would probably lead to a highly inconvenient disturbance.

In particular I am not going to propose that Jack's duty is to approach Jill and say unto her:

" Darling, all that I have is yours. I have no better right to control the income of this establishment than you have. Henceforth we shall share the fund in common, and your word shall be equal to mine."

No! Such a method of curing the woman's legitimate grievance would bring about many bankruptcies and many breaks-up of homes, and most women would probably be worse off than they were before. I would not propose it for various reasons—because evolution does not naturally proceed on these lines, because women have less natural gift for economics than men, because large numbers of women would undoubtedly lose their heads in intoxication, because other large numbers of women would, in my opinion, take a dangerous if not improper advantage of this new privilege, and, finally, because observation has taught me that two people, unless they are very exceptional, cannot successfully run one show. The dual-control device for the enfranchising of women would soon make itself ridiculous.

Legislation is needed to modernise the economic relations between husband and wife, and I have little doubt that with the progress of mankind legislation will ultimately come. Numbers of people will exclaim: "What! Attempt to legislate between husband and wife! Impossible! Moreover, the law, if passed, could never be made operative, and if it were made operative it would destroy the beauty of the conjugal relation." Etc., etc. Nevertheless, the last hundred years has shown a long series of laws which interfere in the conjugal relation, generally for the protection of the wife against husband. Not a great deal has been accomplished, for to this day an English husband has a perfect legal right to cut his wife entirely out of his will and so leave her penniless after his death. This is a survival of barbarism. But something has been accomplished; and the husband has lost some of the tyrannic powers by virtue of which he used to be master in his own house. He cannot, for example, now beat his wife with impunity, nor can he lay hold of her private property, and in sundry other ways his claws have been clipped. Yet every one of those laws was bitterly opposed by reactionary persons who had convinced themselves that if the laws were passed the sacredness of the conjugal relation would be outraged and the decencies of society at an end. Have the laws had the apprehended result? Assuredly not. The laws have had naught but a good result. Husbands have not sulked at them. Wives have not become shrews because of them. Often, of course, the laws have been ignored, disobeyed, trampled on; but in general the menace of them has been effective to curb some of the worst instincts of the human husband, and marriage is thereby decidedly more civilised than it was.

I do not see why a husband should not be compelled by legislation to disclose fully his financial situation to his wife and to allot to her a percentage of his net income for her private and uncontrolled use. "It cannot be done," ten thousand husbands will cry in horror. "I simply cannot afford it." But the cry means nothing at all; it is just an expression of disinclination—the same expression that is heard from employers when sweated employees inconveniently ask for more. Less than a century ago Lancashire cotton masters swore solemnly in public that the cotton trade would be ruined if they were prevented by legislation from working children of twelve years for eighteen hours a day. Such legislation as I have indicated would be good; it would give to the wife a measure of real economic freedom. The average wife would not abuse it, and the average husband, after a few protests, would not resent it. Nor as a rule would he evade it. Matrimony would not be soured. Pessimists may fear that the husband would in practice give only to take back again. I do not think so. The mere social atmosphere of the age would forbid him to do so. A few decades since, if the wife earned money the husband would no doubt have taken even that. But he has learnt better; or, rather, he has been taught better. The wife can now say as positively as the husband: "What's mine's my own." In daily fact the husband does not assume authority over his wife's legal property, whether she happens to have earned it or not. Naturally, if she does earn money the evil of economic slavery is at once greatly ameliorated, if not cured. And herein is an excellent incidental reason why all wives who find themselves with time on their hands should not waste it in parade and morbid reflections, but use it to their own profit and the profit of the community.

There will, however, be no immediate legislation. Haughty husbands may breathe again. Meanwhile the best solution of the existing problem is that husbands should imaginatively put themselves in the place of wives, and act accordingly. Goodwill and an earnest desire to do justice will work more wonders than myriads of laws. At present justice is not being done.

I have tried to prove a case of injustice by married men towards married women. I have another case, not so much of injustice as of lack of sympathy, towards married women in a highly important particular. All women, married or not, over a certain age are the victims of this lack of sympathy, but as the great majority of women over a certain age are married I may confine myself to the married. Not married men alone are the sinners, but the whole of society; and nature herself is against the victims. When Jill married Jack—it is a long time ago now—she had the charm of youth and some beauty. Otherwise the chances are that Jack would not have offered himself as her husband. She was never strikingly beautiful, but in addition to her youthfulness she had an unquestionable physical charm and attractiveness.

In the right light and on the right day and in the right hat she was beautiful. Jack himself considered her beautiful, and would have been ready to quarrel with any swashbuckler who said that she wasn't. A great beauty she was not; neither was she ugly nor in any way repulsive. I am taking her because she was a fair representative average. Lots of men envied Jack when he married her. Jack was delighted with his choice. She had qualities of mind and heart, and Jack had recognised these and was largely depending on them for his future happiness; but what most intoxicated him was the charm of her fresh youth, and of such beauty as was hers. She was a bit of an organiser, for example, but the delicate down on her cheek, her smile, her gestures, her voice, the curves of her features and her arms, Jack reflected more upon these than upon her gift of organising or even upon her moral excellences. And Jill, too, was more proud of these things than of her gift of organising and her moral excellences. Jill exulted in the power which these things gave her.

You may say how wrong Jack and Jill were to attach such importance to these external and transient qualities of Jill. But if you say so, how hypocritical you are. For you yourselves, all of you, recognise or have recognised the potency of just such qualities in other young women. The greatest philosophers have recognised them; and some of the greatest philosophers have done more than recognise them. . . . Those qualities in young women have influenced history constantly and tremendously, and there is no quarter of the world where they do not count. Jack was entirely justified in attaching importance to them, and Jill was entirely justified in taking pride in them and in putting to practical use for her own advantage the power which they gave her. Both Jack and Jill in so doing were obedient to instincts as profound and authentic as any instincts in the whole realm of nature. And if they had acted otherwise they would have been peculiar people and worthy to be held in suspicion and disdain by all those upon whom it has pleased Heaven to bestow a robust common sense.

Well, Jill became a married woman, and for a period those external and transient qualities were enhanced. The bud passed into a radiant flower, and Jill was marvellous. Then the qualities remained stationary. They remained stationary for years. Jack looked at her every morning and he saw no difference in her. Then a difference, an infinitesimal difference, grew apparent, not to Jack but to Jill. Jill detected it before Jack did. Then Jill ceased to mention with satisfaction the number of years she had been married. And if she did mention the number she mentioned it with a slight, uneasy, apologetic laugh. The bloom had vanished from the flower. It was a fine flower, and far, far from being faded; but the bloom had gone. It was a mature flower. Then on Jill's birthdays no reference was made to her age. Jack and Jill in their private conversations did not refer to it. The Jack-and-Jill world had definitely assumed, as an assumption beyond challenging, that Jill was no longer young.

Note that Jill had committed no crime. She had merely suffered a grave misfortune. She has lost, or is losing, through no fault of her own, something very valuable which she once had in plenitude—a power to please, a power to attract, a power to influence. Nevertheless, the general attitude towards her somehow implies that she is in the wrong, and that if she ought not to be blamed she ought at any rate to be scorned. The very men who found pleasure in her lost qualities; and encouraged her to exult in them when she possessed them, despise her because she has lost them. Perhaps Jack does not despise her on this score, for Jack is a loyal fellow, but you may be sure that he despises other women on precisely the same score. And Jill is reproached, though not to her face, because she clings desperately to that which she cannot keep. She actually employs all sorts of devices to help her to maintain a poor pretence. Wicked woman! Childish woman! Can she not see that to do so is absurd? Yet all history is a proof that women deeply experienced in the world will perpetrate follies—yea, and crimes also—in the mad, hopeless, desperate attempt to hold on to privileges which are slipping from them and to which they are no longer entitled. Jill is human. She is in a terrible extremity, and she behaves humanly. Few are they who sympathise with her who is in such real need of sympathy and dare not ask for it. The most horrid word in the vocabulary of a woman is sounding in her ears like a knell—"Forty!" People do not look at her as they used to look at her, nor do they address her in the same way. She sees men turning to girls of a younger generation as once they turned to her. Her mirror, instead of praising, accuses her.

Of course hers is the common lot of women. It is. Toothache is the common lot of both men and women, but we do not disdain a man with toothache, and we do not say to him in his agony: "My dear fellow, why all this fuss? Toothache is the common lot." Death, too, is the common lot, but we do not murmur over the couch of the dying: "After all, yours is the common lot. Be philosophical."

A man dies only once. A woman dies twice. Jill is at her first death. It is a "living death." It usually lasts for several years. With some Jills it lasts till the second and final death. Meanwhile old Jack is jogging along as usual, or probably rather better than usual. His attractiveness has not diminished. He mentions his age with relish. He has nothing to fear from birthdays. He may not be so active as he was, but his golf is improving, and I doubt whether he ever had a better time.

There are compensations for Jill, it is said. The compensation of acquired wisdom. The compensation of calmer pulses. The compensation of children. She is said to "live again in her children." And so on. Phrases! Phrases! Every age has its compensations—partial compensations. But for a woman there is no full and genuine compensation for the departure of beauty and freshness. Nothing can compensate even for a vanished complexion. Nothing! And I assert that the most devoted mothers, the most spiritual women, the women who live most for others, have felt acutely the secret pangs of the vanishing of a complexion. Naturally Jill must make the best of her compensations. She must abandon the things which are impermanent and embrace the permanent. She must exist on a higher plane. This particular Jill may be able to do so. But there are many Jills who simply cannot; Jills who are appointed by destiny to be pretty and charming and young, and whom destiny has pushed into the world without other resources. We all know such Jills. What about them? All Jills, during the period of woman's first death, deserve treatment infinitely respectful and sympathetic. They don't get it. Their tragedy is unnoticed. And men, in the incredible baseness of their masculinity, say carelessly among themselves in discussing Jill: "She's getting a bit long in the tooth."

CHAPTER SEVEN: THE SOCIAL INTERCOURSE BUSINESS

CHAPTER SEVEN

THE SOCIAL INTERCOURSE BUSINESS

IF society were not kept together by conscious and constant effort it would fall apart into small and still smaller groups, until discomfort, anarchy, eccentricity and solitariness gradually ate the heart out of civilisation. Man may be a gregarious animal; but he is also an exclusive, unclubbable and critical animal, very apt to throw a brick at a stranger simply because the fellow is a stranger. Happily, he has discovered that gregariousness, or the habit of mixing and joining forces, pays; it brings order, justice, liberty, wisdom, security, comfort and pleasure to the units which combine, in a degree that would be impossible if they did not combine; and the history of the human race is the history of its combinations to this or that end.

Most of the agencies, however, which depend upon combination, and therefore encourage combination, do not regard intercourse as an end, but as a means. The churches draw units to units and thus promote intercourse, but their aim goes far beyond mortal institutions, which, indeed, they expressly disdain. Civil government is a tremendous integrating force, but its object is to procure order, justice, and (in theory, if not in practice) the individual liberty of the unit. Armies bring men closer together than any other device invented by the wit of man, but they are for defence—and sometimes for conquest; assuredly not for intercourse! Schools and universities employ intercourse in the machinery of instruction. Trade knits up a nation, and one nation with another, more effectively and permanently than anything else, but the intention of trade is to get personal gain by satisfying the wants of another. Sport is of two kinds: the murderous, which organises for killing; and the innocuous, which seeks the physical fitness of the individual and harmlessly ministers to the spirit of emulation and the almost universal desire to win. Philanthropy creates association, but as a rule for neither mutual interest nor mutual help, the interest and help being usually confined to those who are outside the association, which within is often characterised by mutual scorn and jealousy.

All the aforementioned activities (save, rarely, the murderous form of sport) are social activities which help to keep society together, which in fact imperiously insist on cohesion, but none of them is primarily interested in intercourse as such. They are all either too grandiose, too practical, too egotistic, or too mean to think about intercourse for the pure sake of intercourse.

There is, however, a social activity whose sole aim is intercourse between human beings, with no avowed ulterior purpose, an activity of which intercourse is the end and not the means. This activity has, so far as I am aware, no name. In the uppermost circles it is vaguely called by the Press "society doings," an unpleasing description. It is found at its most elaborate and complete in those circles, and as we descend in the social scale its significance decreases until in the lowest ranks we find it quite unorganised and left to chance.

This activity is a healthy one and essential to the well-being of the community. It springs from, and is a direct expression of, the gregarious instinct. It is the outcome of a characteristic almost invariably to be discovered in sane, sagacious, well-balanced individuals—namely, curiosity concerning other people. All right-thinking individuals are "interested in people." They want to know what people are "like," what they think, what they do, what their habits are—and their weaknesses. They want to enjoy them, to learn from them, to teach them. Social gossip is everywhere popular because it gratifies a fundamental need of the heart; and those who condemn it are either affected or queer in the head.

The whole business of organised social intercourse is an extremely important function of the community—how important may be appreciated by imagining what the state would be if it were suddenly suppressed. To sneer at it as conventional and futile shows a serious failure of understanding. It is no more futile than mortar in a wall is futile; and conventional it must be in form, for it could not be organised without conventions, and if it were not organised it could not accomplish its work, even badly.

The significant thing about it is that it is

mainly in the hands of women. Women are responsible for it, and theirs must be the credit or the blame attaching to it. The general verdict upon the handling of it is adverse, and properly so. Women have not thus far earned the esteem of mankind for their achievement in this their own sphere; and the judgments of mankind are usually rather sound. We cannot now examine the entire organisation of social intercourse throughout all ranks of society; but we can at any rate examine it in the rank which leads, which is the imitated exemplar for the other ranks, and whose influence is traceable everywhere.

The mere material machinery of the huge enterprise is simple and good. Nothing, for instance, could be more efficient for its purpose than the system of paying and receiving calls, which is seen at its best in a country neighbourhood and which ensures a fair and equal social opportunity for all newcomers and strangers within the caste. It is the spirit animating the machinery that is wrong.

Let me say at once that I do not blame the institution of caste. Class-distinctions are the product of a powerful and ineradicable instinct in man. They have always obtained and they always will. Different classes never mix well in pure sociableness. The basis of class distinctions may change. At one time they rested on birth. At another on birth and wealth. At another on wealth alone. At present birth, wealth, fame and artistic attainment all have a share in the determination of class distinctions. Other changes may follow. But class distinctions will certainly persist until the sun has ceased to warm the earth to the point of being habitable. Hence I would not upbraid the leaders of society because they pay due attention to that which cannot possibly be ignored. (Nevertheless, I will here interject the remark that there is a difference between a regard for class distinctions and snobbishness.)

My first charge against the women who lead society is that they do not comprehend the importance of social intercourse in the life of the community. They have no philosophical foundation for what they do. They share the common illusion that what they do is futile, and they do it because it is correct, because it distracts them, because it saves them from the tedium of eternal idleness. They may sometimes do it from a sense of duty, but of the reason of the duty they have no conception, except occasionally the narrow and unworthy conception that it helps their husbands' masculine schemes.

Next, the vocabulary of the business must be arraigned. There is perhaps no better criticism of any activity than its vocabulary and manner of speech. I would not take exception to a moderate use of slang nor to a moderate amount of bad grammar. Slang is like a tonic to a language. And as grammar is simply not taught with effectiveness in the best schools, one ought not to be surprised or hurt when the greatest dames utter such sad phrases as "Let my husband and I help in some way."

The real vice of the fashionable vocabulary is that it abounds far too much in superlatives, which superlatives are intended to emphasize the two emotions of gratitude and pleasure. I can remember the time when a hostess was content to say: "It was very good of you to come." She didn't mean it even then. She meant: "It was very good of me to ask you to come." But she did utter her polite phrase with a certain decency and a certain air of conviction. Then some woman discovered that "very" was not emphatic enough, and said: "It was awfully good of you to come." "Awful" is a serious word, and needs some elocution to carry it off successfully. It did not last long. "Frightfully" took its place, but nobody could give "frightfully" the right intonation, and so to-day "most frightfully" is employed. "It was most frightfully good of you to come." "It was most frightfully good of you to ask me." The greatest actress in the world could not make the phrase sound real after a tea-party, and hostesses and guests do not attempt to make it sound real. They pour it out anyhow, turning a smile on and off as if by a tap. They will, in the quite misguided effort to be convincing, soon be compelled to invent a phrase more frightful than "most frightfully." And so the cycle will continue until someone discovers that there is naught so unemphatic as over-emphasis, and superlatives will go under for a period.

In the meantime it is impossible for anyone to do anything for anyone else in this high world without being drenched in a treacle of thanksgivings. If you strike a match for a woman with an unlighted cigarette, your ear will hear, between puffs, words of gratitude which would be appropriate if you had saved her only babe from drowning. The phenomenon, silly in itself, is significant as an unmistakable index of general silliness.

We will pass from the vocabulary to the entertainment itself. Take a dinner. Let it be of medium size, say a dozen covers. You may not be acquainted with half the guests, and the chances are ten to one against your being introduced. Such is the custom at the affairs whose theoretical aim is to promote intercourse! You are lucky if you know your neighbour's name. But of one thing you may be sure—the company will be composed chiefly of persons whom it is a crime not to know. Often it will be composed exclusively of such persons. No arrangement is less likely to result in sociability. All the people in the party feel in the hinterland of their minds that the affair is organised for the after-glory of the hostess and in no way for the general benefit.

The conversation before dinner is irregular, sporadic, and perfunctory. You sit down to table, and then suddenly, as soon as the first dish is served, a tremendous outbreak of chatter occurs. The din is deafening, because six different conversations are proceeding at once in a very small space, and each is fighting against the disturbing noise of the others. The hostess answers the chief guest with a somewhat pre-occupied air; she is drinking in the sound of the enormous babble —the proof that her dinner is "going" and that the obligation to talk glibly and endlessly at dinner is being faithfully observed by all her guests. The tongues of the diners seem to be driven forward by the ruthless force of the obligation, and by the ambition of the hostess, so that the meal becomes a secondary matter; and under a kind of sinister enchantment, in a dream, in a trance, the guests eat and drink whatever is thrust at them, their eyes saying: "Anything will do. I am busy and can only snatch mouthfuls at intervals." But, of course, there is no interchange of real thoughts; all real thoughts hide themselves in terror amid the fracas. Occasionally one individual may by mastery seize the whole table, but he cannot hold it. Neither the host nor the hostess attempts any direction. They have created a monster, and they watch it, helplessly.

After the savoury, the women go. The women smoke and drink coffee and liqueurs in one room. The men smoke and drink coffee and liqueurs in another. The only difference between the two assemblies is the difference between cigarettes and cigars. The extent of this separation of the sexes (which in France is properly eschewed as being barbaric) depends upon hazard. In the provinces it is lengthier than in capitals; indeed, in the provinces it may endure to the end of the evening.

Upon the reunion of the sexes in the drawing-room the inexperienced hope for some renewal of vigour on a plane of calm intelligence. The hope is vain. The experienced know well enough that energy is exhausted and the evening virtually over. The guests one by one depart in iridescent clouds of superlatives, and none among them can honestly say more than this: " I have eaten something." None among them can satisfactorily answer the questions: "Why did I come? What advantage beyond an appeased stomach have I gained by the adventure? Why do hostesses give dinners?" The fact is that the hostess had thought of everything except a plan of intercourse. She had provided an opera of which the sole libretto was the menu of the dinner; and even the meal itself was impaired by the anarchy which she had taken no precautions to control.

The leaders of society make a practice of combining social intercourse with the encouragement of artists and the furtherance of art. As, for instance, in the musical "At Home." The musical "At Home" is an excellent invention; and ought, skilfully executed, to achieve much finer social results than any mere meal; for it puts a premium on the things of the spirit and averts attention from the body's gross desires. Surely it is better for a human being to have even a surfeit of songs by Schumann than to take over-much roast goose and ingurgitate too many liqueurs.

Admirable "talent" is usually engaged for these solemnities; genius itself may be hired for them. The dainties offered make the mouth of the eager inexperienced simpleton water. He arrives shortly after the hour indicated on the card, and finds a handful of people in the vast drawing-room. The hostess says: "How sweet of you to come so early!" In another forty minutes the room is comfortably full, and the concert begins. It is bedtime by rights. A singer sings. At the close of the first verse there are ecstatic murmurs of adoration. New guests are continually entering. They surge inwards in an almost unceasing procession, and produce a considerable amount of noise in their prodigious efforts to be noiseless. They greet their innumerable friends in the assemblage, unaware that nods and smiles may be nearly as disturbing as talk and footfalls. At the close of the song the applause, while maintaining the character of true refinement, is frenzied. Agitated listeners, who a moment earlier had been saluting all over the apartment, surround the artist and give him to understand that there never was, is not, and never could be anybody like him, and that the pleasure he affords is so acute as to be well nigh dangerous to life. The artist may or may not be nauseated; none can tell; but he is amiable and evidently tries to think of something fresh to say in response.

More guests are continually entering. The room which was comfortably full is now uncomfortably full. The supply of chairs and sofas is long since exhausted. Chatter is terrific, and the movement of fans adds to the sensation of restlessness. An awe-struck "Shoo!" from somewhere near the piano brings about a semi-silence, which gradually and with great difficulty becomes three-quarter silence. Another artist sets to work. Few can see him, but many want to know who he is; for the hostess has omitted to provide a platform, and the artist is compelled to do what he can out of the midst of a jungle of panting fellow creatures. The same happens to him as happened to his predecessor. He, too, is the greatest that ever was, is, or could conceivably be.

So the affair unfolds itself. Guests are still happily entering. Beautiful and elegant women now sit on the floor. The multitude is such that if it were in a theatre or hall the licensing authority would prosecute the lessee for over-crowding, and firemen would tremble in their helmets at the thought of the consequences of a cry of "Fire." Music succeeds to music, and rapture to rapture; but in fact the body has after all conquered the spirit, and the rapture grows more and more mechanical, for the physical conditions of existence at the "At Home" have become the secret preoccupation of everybody—except the hostess. Look at the hostess, standing in everlasting welcome near the door. Is she distressed by that which she has brought to pass? Not so. She is radiant. She is triumphant. She has obtained the best artists and there is the biggest crush in her rooms that ever was. The hour is her apotheosis.

By the exercise of brutal and disregarding strength you approach the door. "Must you go? So early? So sorry! How delightful to see you here! Do have something before you go." You force yourself down the stairs, overpowering an upward stream of arrivals. In the corners of the stairs people are holding converse, not about music or any other art. You pass the doors of a room full of eaters and drinkers and tinkling with laughter; and as you extricate your hat and coat from a thousand others you hear from above the faint, far sound of more music. The sound is pathetic. It somehow makes your eyes water by the pathos of it. You emerge into the cool street. As far as the eye can see stretches a line of illuminated vehicles with their attendants. And they are not pathetic.

So much for the encouragement of music and the promotion of intelligent social intercourse by the leaders of society with all the machinery of opulence at their disposal. These women are indefatigable in their attention to music not only privately but in public. As soon as they have convinced themselves that an operatic season or a season of ballet, for example, deserves on artistic grounds to succeed, and is likely to succeed, they will all be godmothers to the affair. They will buy the most expensive seats, and will do their utmost to ensure the success upon which they count. They even attend the performances. It is true that they invariably arrive late, that they have an air of owning the theatre, that they treat the boxes as drawing-rooms and visit one another in those drawing-rooms and talk loudly therein, and gesticulate to their friends across the auditorium, that they applaud rhapsodically what they have not listened to, and that they leave early, having acutely exasperated the rest of the audience. Nevertheless, they attend the performances and set the true seal of correctness on the performances; and incidentally, of course, they have shown the humbler world what is the proper attitude towards art.

Their method with young painters is naturally different. It has to be. But it has this in common with the other method—it ensures publicity and glory for themselves. They never "adopt" a painter who is not a portrait-painter, and when they have adopted a portrait-painter they insist on his painting portraits of themselves. They pay him well. They show him off. They send up his prices. They give him more work than he can do. They are sometimes nice to his wife. They flatter him. But he must flatter them—on canvas. The sequel is in nearly every case that on the wave of commercial and social triumph he is overtaken by artistic ruin, and he knows it. . . . Unnecessary for me to pursue this vein further.

* * *

No! The women who lead society are not the most stupid, snobbish, self-seeking women on the face of the planet. Talk to them when they are not engaged in their great and magnificent business of giving or receiving hospitality in a spectacular manner, and you find that they often have an intelligent grasp of social, political, and artistic questions, that they feel genuine emotions of their own about these questions, and that they desire to act for the general good. Further, they are even aware that they have responsibilities towards the community. Nor are they in a special degree snobbish. Most people are snobbish at any rate. I never yet met anyone who was not. Snobbishness is not a new vice peculiar to this present epoch. (There was, if one can correctly read between the lines of authentic accounts, a good deal of it among the ancient Hebrews). On the contrary, snobbishness seems to be somewhat on the decrease, doubtless owing to the spread of the democratic principle, which surely renders indulgence in the cruder forms of snobbishness rather perilous, because unfashionable. As for a charge of self-seeking, self-seeking of some kind is nearly as universal as snobbishness, and it is far more defensible. Moreover, self-seeking need interfere with the enterprise of proper social leadership no more than it interferes with any other enterprise.

Social leadership is badly done not in the least because the leaders want personal glory in large quantities, but because they have not understood the possibilities of what they are about. If they chose to put more brains into their work they might easily double the harvest of personal glory, for nothing but thoughtlessness prevents them from earning the applause of the multitudes of sensible plain persons who now, while perhaps envying, sneer at and deride them. The leaders are inefficient, and they cannot urge the excuse of the average human being for this human defect, because their opportunities are unique; they have the choice of the finest social material that the community offers, and considerations of monetary expense do not, for a good reason, hamper any of their schemes.

There are two things which the women whom destiny has called to lead the social body might do at once to improve the whole structure of intercourse. The first is to get rid of the nauseating atmosphere of exaggerated insincerity which renders it ridiculous. I do not advocate that they should immediately and drastically adopt the habit of speaking nothing but the truth to their guests and their hosts. Truth is a dangerous commodity, and ought to be employed accordingly. If it were not half-veiled and sometimes hidden entirely in a tinsel of smooth phrases, intercourse, instead of being ameliorated, would be brought to an end. But in this matter there is a medium between the harsh directness of ruthless and unimaginative egotists and the soft sawdust of flatterers who are determined to be agreeable at a cheap rate and by the tongue only. Common sense, the general verdict of mankind, will and always does indicate that medium. The present generation has lost it, and seems to be going further and further away from it.

Again, though some verbal insincerity is

essential to the maintenance of friendliness, such insincerity should be performed with skill, with due care, and with a real desire to achieve what it theoretically sets out to achieve. The insincerities of to-day are performed with a negligent and cynical clumsiness which must astound the detached observer. They fulfil no good purpose; they are a canker at the root of the honesty of relationships. A reform of vocabulary would automatically involve a reform of tone and style, with the result of changing for the better the entire structure of intercourse from top to bottom.

The second thing concerns the attitude of society towards the arts. Anglo-Saxon communities do not respect the arts as do, for instance, Latin communities. The defect is admitted, notorious. Intelligent individuals everywhere lament it. Here is a work of social advancement which lies ready to the hand of social leaders. But social leaders, many of whom in private fully appreciate the potential significance of the arts in the life of the community, seldom do anything but *patronize* art, treat it as a toy, as an adjunct, as a mere tool convenient for the spectacular glorification of their personal activities. While using it, they openly flout it—certainly do not show the slightest respect for it. The opportunity awaits them to raise all the arts to their proper place in the social fabric; for snobbishness, which upon occasion has high uses, would ensure that their example was imitated. They have not the wit to take the opportunity. Yet if they did they would acquire more renown and prestige than all existing practices secure for them.

Turning to the broad aspect of social intercourse as conducted by the leaders, the following criticisms are obvious. Too much is undertaken. Not only are the "functions," as they are called, too numerous, but they are, as a rule, too large in scale. They are done wholesale, and size and number seem to count more than anything else. They result in exhaustion and *ennui*. They are too frequently regarded as an unavoidable bore. And while in many respects physical luxury is absurdly over-accentuated, mere physical comfort is often glaringly neglected. Moreover, the gatherings themselves are wrongly composed, in that the great axiom that you *can* have too much of a good thing is neglected. Twelve celebrated talkers at a dinner of twelve will infallibly ruin that dinner.

And, what is still more important, ideas are not taken into account and the gatherings are not directed. I am not suggesting that hostesses should give to their parties a didactic tendency with a conscious aim of social improvement. I am willing to admit that the paramount end should be the mere pleasure of human intercourse. I am ready to leave to special circles (where the craft of sociableness is clumsier even than it is in general circles) the conscious cultivation and spreading of special ideas. I will allow that hostesses must arrange things for the aid of the sublime institution of marriage, and that a proportion of gatherings have to be, and ought to be, simply frivolous and bereft of all intellectuality. But I hold that in the main human beings are interesting to one another by reason of their ideas, and therefore that you will not get the best intercourse, and the most satisfying pleasure, unless you provide conditions which favour the smooth and full exchange of ideas. In the large majority of cases hostesses collect the raw majority of good intercourse and just waste it, leave it lying about, sterilise it, strangle it, stun it, or offend it into perfect futility. They do not realise that, bar miracles of chance, nothing excellent is produced without creative thought. And they do not think creatively in the region of ideas. If they gave half as much preliminary reflection to the circulation of ideas as they give to the circulation of high-class food and wines they would achieve intercourse which would positively change the colour of society and multiply beyond computing the zest of life. They have not understood. They have misunderstood. They are still victimised by the singular delusion that ideas are the enemy of joy. . . . Not that I would have them take a metaphorical baton and openly conduct their assemblies as a conductor conducts an orchestra. We are in the twentieth century, not in the eighteenth; and the twentieth must be more subtle than the eighteenth. It is; only hostesses have not kept abreast of civilisation. That is all. The future is to women. In this affair of social intercourse the field, as in the past, is peculiarly theirs. And five hundred of them in any country might, if they could summon up their dormant intelligence, revolutionise the social life of that country. We are yet only at the beginning of intercourse.

CHAPTER EIGHT: MASCULINE VIEW OF THE SEX DISCORD

CHAPTER EIGHT

MASCULINE VIEW OF THE SEX DISCORD

EXAMPLE is said to be better than precept. Here, in a somewhat different sense of the word, is an example. It may seem trivial. It is not really trivial. It illustrates the "dailiness" of married life in an average successful marriage. It shows, perhaps more clearly than any amount of aphorisms, epigrams, or saws that I could invent, the nature of the sex discord, and if the contemplation of it aids mutual understanding in husbands and wives, then it may indeed be better than the best precept. The matter with precepts is that they are not concrete, and that when a crisis arises, either they seem not to be applicable or they cannot in practice be applied.

It was an important day (for a reason which will appear) in the married life of Jack and Jill. These two had matured. They had also prospered. For a year past they had been living at a "place" (small, but still a "place") in the country which Jack had acquired on advantageous terms out of his accumulated reserves. They were sitting together after lunch. Seeing the importance of the day Jack had decided not to "go in" [to town]. He could afford these caprices. There was not a cloud in the deep-blue conjugal sky. There was no sign of a cloud. An unspecked firmament of calm felicity arched the pair over.

Suddenly Jill said in a casual tone:

"I hope you aren't going to let Snagge compete in the chrysanthemum show this year."

Snagge was the head gardener.

"Why not?" asked Jack cautiously.

"Well, why should he?" she parried. "It isn't as if he hadn't got plenty to do without fiddling around his precious prize-winning chrysanthemums all day. He neglects lots of things. You aren't here, of course, and you don't know."

Now as, according to the terms of the unwritten conjugal treaty, the garden had been made Jack's special province, Jack did not care for these remarks, which implied, first, that he was not doing his job properly, and, second, that Snagge was hoodwinking him. The second implication was more unpleasant than the first. However, perceiving that conjugal friction on such an important day would be unseemly as well as inconvenient, Jack maintained all his self-possession and said in a placatory manner:

"Everyone in the district seems to think old Snagge does very well. And you know he went in for chrysanthemums long before we came here; and——"

"Still," Jill interrupted sweetly, "the place *is* ours, isn't it? It isn't his."

"Quite so," Jack handsomely concurred. "But when we took him on we knew he had always specialised in chrysanths. They say he's the best hand at them anywhere near here. And he won the silver medal for us last year."

"Yes," said Jill. "And you let him keep it. It's got your name on and it's hung up in his cottage. He does what he likes with you, Snagge does."

Said Jack, nicely but firmly:

"It was I who suggested that he should keep the medal. He won it. I didn't. I couldn't grow a prize chrysanthemum to save my life. *He* certainly never suggested keeping it. In fact, he didn't want to keep it."

"Yes," said Jill with benevolent condescension. "He's very clever that way."

"What way?"

"Oh! Never mind." Jill laughed.

Jack reflected:

"How childishly suspicious women are!" He went on aloud: "We've got to remember that flower shows are his interest in life. It would be rather hard lines on him to cut 'em off. Why should we?"

Jill arose and looked through the open window on Snagge's domain.

"He's not trimmed the edge of the lawn again this week," said she, as if she had but just observed this phenomenon of neglect.

"I know," said Jack quickly. "I told him if he had to choose between trimming the edges and giving the lawn a good roll after the rain he must do the rolling."

"I've not noticed him doing any special rolling," said Jill. "And I spend a lot of time in the garden weeding and trying to keep things tidy. One or two people have kindly given me some nasty polite hints about little details in the garden. People do notice things. But of course if Snagge really must spend all his time in getting ready for flower-shows, I suppose something's got to suffer. I can't see the object of flower-shows myself. They take the gardeners off their work for months, and in the end it means two men's time for at least three days. Besides the expense of cartage, and so on. Not to mention the subscription to the Society. And all the best blooms taken away instead of being in my drawing-room! And for what, I should like to know."

"But, my child," Jack reasoned with her grandly, "flower-shows play a very important part in the development of horticulture."

"They don't play a very important part in the development of my garden!" cried Jill.

"*Her* garden!" thought Jack. "And has she forgotten what day it is? She cannot have forgotten. *Perhaps she is taking advantage of the day to get her own way.*"

Nevertheless, though his thoughts ran thus, he kept them to himself. He even kept them out of his expression and out of his voice as he placidly continued:

"Yes, my child, indirectly they do help

the development of your garden." (It would have been easy to put a sarcastic accent on the word "your," but Jack refrained.) "Flower-shows encourage good horticulture through rivalry. And if it hadn't been for flower-shows there's many a fine variety—of rose, for instance—that would never have come into existence at all. Flower-shows mean the spread of expert knowledge. And it's a social duty for everybody who has a garden to do what he can to help flower-shows. Besides," he added, "what would people say if we dropped out—with a garden like ours?" He was cleverly appealing to Jill's characteristic feminine sensitiveness about "what people would say."

"And yet," Jill retorted with unconcealed sarcasm, "you're always at me for minding what people say! That's just like a man, that is!"

"All right, infant! All right!" said Jack, magnificently magnanimous, and he gave a gentle laugh. "But you must understand I've practically promised to compete this year, anyhow." And he arose and walked out, and lit a cigarette. The conjugal firmament was thick with gathering clouds.

Thank goodness he had checked them by his well-known mixture of tact and firmness. He had silenced Jill, and the danger of a storm was at any rate averted for the present. Exasperating, incredible woman, Jill! All women were exasperating and incredible. Must treat 'em like kids. . . . She had no feeling for old Snagge's feelings. To be forbidden flower-shows would be an absolute tragedy for old Snagge. She couldn't see it! Or wouldn't! Probably wouldn't. Perhaps it was a case of couldn't; because women had no real imagination. She couldn't even see the utility of flower-shows. But, of course, women *couldn't* see things like that. And then they were so absurdly suspicious—always attributing "motives," and always thinking that their husbands were being done in the eye. . . . Yet attributing guile to their husbands! . . .

How cheap, how very cheap, of her to use the phrase "Just like a man." Never, never, had he said to her "Just like a woman." No! He could not stoop to such a reply.

The most serious thing was her disregard of the day and what was due to it. A ruthless disregard! She didn't appear to care a whit whether, on that great day, they quarrelled or not. No! She had an idea in her head, and everything else must give in to it. Strange, how mistresses and gardeners never "get on" together!

He came across old Snagge near the potting-shed.

"Well, Snagge," he greeted the man jovially, "how are the chrysanths shaping? Making their wood all right?" (He relished the technical phrase which he had picked up from Snagge himself.)

"They're making their wood all right, sir," asserted Snagge. "But missis tells me this morning as you don't think of showing this year."

* * *

The storm seemed to burst like a clap of thunder right overhead in the conjugal firmament. The duplicity of the woman! The infernal cheek of the woman! Had it not been solemnly agreed that he, Jack, had control of the garden? And here she had gone behind his back, and, attributing to him a wish that was the exact contrary of his real wish, she had practically given an order to the gardener. She had confronted him, Jack, with a *fait accompli.* Yes, it was incredible.

What could he do? He could not say to Snagge: "Your mistress is an unprincipled liar," though he had a most powerful desire to make some such remark. Nor could he decently intimate to the gardener in any way that a conflict of opinion existed between himself and Jill. He just said, very awkwardly:

"Oh, no! Oh, no! I didn't mean that. Your mistress must have misunderstood me." And he walked off.

"Well," he reflected, "if she wants a row she must have it. She's got no shadow of an excuse." An exciting and horrible sensation came over him. He knew what that sensation meant.

Later in the afternoon the boy arrived home from his first term at a big public school. It was this prodigious event that rendered the day so important. The majority of spirited husbands and spirited wives quarrel, at intervals. And the solemn fact that they have become fathers and mothers and ought to set an example to growing lads at public schools will not prevent them from quarrelling. Yet surely Jill ought to have known better than to risk a quarrel on the very day that the boy resumed possession of his parents after the first separation. Surely a sense of decency ought to have restrained her. But women have no sense of decency. So thought Jack as they welcomed the boy.

Jill's demeanour towards the boy was a perfect harmony of stateliness and affection. Her kiss was a maternal masterpiece. Jack sincerely admired it. Then came Jack's turn to greet the boy. Now there existed between Jack and the boy a kind of male freemasonry, under the rules of which they always falsely pretended that they had no particular interest in each other. Jack in defence of this humbug had once made Jill angry by asserting that necessarily a deep gulf separated parents from their children, and that this gulf never had been and never would be bridged—at any rate, by the parents. Jack greeted the boy in the traditional manner, and both males winked.

"Oh, dear!" Jill exclaimed, seriously protesting. "Why do you encourage him to be callous? He's callous enough without that. This terrible callousness will be the death of me. Johnnie, you really ought to show more respect for your father."

"A strange outbreak!" thought Jack, but the boy evidently attached no significance to it. The boy just said:

"Go it, mater!" and touched her chin with his hard, dirty hand, and she smiled as if she could not help smiling. It was not tact on Johnnie's part, it was merely careless instinct.

These two soon went upstairs together, side by side, seemingly as thick as thieves, the idea being that Jill was to display to the boy his glorified bedroom, which he had been "promised."

Jack was left solitary below. He did not quite like being left solitary; he thought it was a bit rough on him; but for the first half-hour he was content enough; and, in fact, rather pleased that both he and Jill had by admirable acting successfully concealed from the boy the miserable truth that they were at war. But when half an hour had stretched into an hour and an hour into an hour and a half he began to be annoyed. Did Jill exclusively own the boy? (He was too proud to go up to them.) Then the boy descended, but not Jill. Father and son did not find a lot to say to each other. They never did. They carried on their interminable game of callousness and everything was all right.

At dinner Jill, beautifully dressed, showed her best histrionic form. Nobody could have guessed that she and Jack were at war. (But *did* the boy guess?) She insisted on the boy being conversational. And Jack loyally supported her, though his sympathies were with the boy, who was only thirteen. How on earth could she reasonably expect the boy to give a connected and diverting conversational description of the atmosphere of school?

In a somewhat disconcerting gap in the talk Jack gallantly did his duty, and broached a new subject in a semi-facetious vein.

"And what were you and your mother plotting together all that time upstairs?" he gaily asked.

Jill said naught.

"Oh! Nothing!" said the boy. "She was looking through my clothes, that's all."

When the coffee was served, the boy took some sugar and unfortunately omitted to pass the bowl on to his mother. Then Jill spoke, quite quietly. She said:

"Johnnie, I'm waiting for the sugar. I wish you'd remember that you aren't at school; you're at home. You really must be more thoughtful for others. You're only a boy—recollect that. *If your father never thinks of anybody but himself,* that's no reason why you should be the same. Your father is your father."

The words were so staggering to Jack that he did not at first feel their full force. As for the boy, the boy accepted all the words with indifference.

"Oh! Sorry!" he murmured casually, and passed the sugar.

* * *

Jill sent the boy to bed early. She said he looked pale and tired. The boy, having separately tapped every pane of glass in the enormous Chippendale bookcase that adorned the drawing-room—apparently in obedience to some privately vowed rite—dutifully departed. His mother followed him after a second or so, calling out to him that she would see him tucked up. In another few seconds she announced over the stair-rail to Jack, the drawing-room door being open:

"I shan't come down again, Jack. Good night."

"Good night," growled Jack with savagery. He was alone on the ground-floor with his grievance and his great secret anger. The exciting and terrible sensation of the early afternoon now entirely obsessed him. Briefly, he was in an acute state of fury against the unexampled female wretch who happened to be his wife. He was determined to establish justice in that house, boy or no boy, rupture or no rupture, be the cost what it might.

The woman was utterly impossible. She had gone to bed, but she could not escape him. He would listen for her to leave the boy's room, and as soon as she had gone into her own room he would ascend and challenge her and destroy her pretensions for ever and ever. He listened and waited and listened. Not a sound! Seeing that the boy was tired, and that she had sent him to bed, it was very illogical of her to stay gossiping with him so long. Just like her, however!

Then he heard the expected sound of the boy's bedroom door opening and closing, and he started up, eager for battle.

He had scarcely got to the door of the drawing-room when he saw the flounce of Jill's skirts on the stairs. Naturally, having stated that she should not come down again, she was coming down again! Naturally! He rushed back to his easy-chair, and seized the evening paper, which he had already read through without understanding a word of it, and gazed at it as though it were an enthralling *chef d'œuvre* of literature. Jill came just inside the door.

"Jack," she said coldly, "I want to speak to you."

"Yes," he said terribly. "And *I* want to speak to *you.*"

"If you'll just let me speak," she went on. "I think I ought to warn you against trying to make me look small before the boy. I dare say you don't mean it, but you don't reflect. You suggested to-night that I had been "plotting" with him. It may seem a small thing, but it shows what you think of me. Plotting against whom? I could only be plotting against you. What must the boy think when he hears things like that? Not that I mind so much for myself, but you give the boy the idea that I don't really respect your authority—how could I if I plot? And so *he* is not likely to respect your authority. Now what I want above all else is that he *should* respect your authority. He needs authority at home. You *would* have him go to a public school, but it isn't an unmixed good. I hope you don't mind me speaking to you."

Jack had thought that he knew all the possibilities of Jill's dissembling nature; but he now admitted to himself that he had underestimated it. The wondrous guile of the woman! Oh! She had genuinely surprised him. She had quite upset his plan of campaign. She had taken him in flank.

"You know perfectly well that I was joking, perfectly well!" he almost shouted, with all his wild resentment unloosed.

"You ought to give notice when you're going to joke," she said with coolness. "Otherwise how are we to tell! Nobody could have guessed."

He flamed higher.

"And I suppose it was to strengthen my authority with the boy that you said I never think of anyone but myself!" His tone was like a hatchet swung by a madman. "A nice infernal lie to tell to the boy!"

"So you *do* never think of anyone but yourself!" said Jill. "I'm not complaining about it. You're the most important person in the house, and I should be the last to complain. But I don't want the boy to grow like you—if I can help it."

"And there's another thing," Jack slashed about him with barbaric power. "There's another thing! Why do you go and tell Snagge behind my back that I've decided not to exhibit chrysanthemums this year, when you know jolly well I haven't decided any such thing? A pretty state of affairs! If I went into your kitchen and gave orders to your servants against your wishes, I know what sort of fuss there'd be. You must be mad!"

Jill answered frigidly:

"I gave no orders to Snagge. As a fact, Snagge ignores me. I might be a visitor instead of the mistress. If I pick a flower he glares at me. Now, now!" Jack was about to burst forth again. "Please don't get excited. You know you'll only have a bad night if you do."

She went away.

In that detail, at any rate, she was correct. He did have a sleepless night. At three o'clock in the morning, when the earliest birds were beginning to discuss the question of victuals, his active mind was revolving in the same circle for the hundredth thousandth time. "She agrees to the garden being managed by me—indeed, she implored me to manage it. Then she interferes. Can't answer my arguments. Never could. Gets cross. Obstinate as a mule. And all the time she'd been to Snagge beforehand and told him he wasn't to exhibit. What *can* a fellow do with such a woman? I'm hanged if I know! Then I'm dashed if she doesn't outrageously insult me in front of the boy. Never think of anyone but myself? Why, I'm always thinking of her, always giving way to her ridiculous whims! And then instead of apologising she sticks to it; and, what's more, she accuses me of insulting *her!* And see how she had monopolised the boy to-day! This will have to stop. I shan't have it. . . ."

He foresaw separation, and divorce. Of course, the existence of the boy would complicate matters, but that couldn't be helped. The situation must be faced. Positively he should not yield about the flower-show. And yet, how effective it would be to yield, to say in an aggrieved, philosophic tone to her: "What can I do? If you choose to behave in this way there's no more to be said. I am certainly not going to Snagge and tell him that my orders are different from yours and he must take mine. That is not my way. It may be yours, but it is not mine."

Yes, that would be very effective. But no! He would never yield. Throughout the day she had behaved outrageously. On no point could she justify herself. . . . Separation. . . . Yes, freedom!

* * *

He was wakened up by the familiar prolonged creak of his bedroom door. He knew at once that he had unexpectedly gone to sleep in the midst of his vast grievances and must have overslept himself. The door was slowly opening. He saw the figure of his wife. She was dressed in white. She was smiling. She looked extraordinarily young and girlish for the mother of a boy aged thirteen. She looked as fresh as a flower in the freshness of the morning. She was carrying a glass of fresh flowers. The boy followed her. They were both of them tiptoeing and half laughing, like delicious conspirators. The boy was carrying the terrier. The terrier, recognising her master's bed, which was her bed in the morning, gave a leap, and in an instant had disappeared under the bed-clothes and was burrowing her way beneath them to the foot of the bed. Jill placed the glass of flowers on the night table, and then she put her cool hand on Jack's brow, like a nurse, inquiringly, anxious and yet reassuring.

The grievances of the martyrised husband seemed to melt away like snow. He tried to maintain them in being, and could not. She was a monster, but she was Jill, and she was so fresh; and her alluringness was so high above argument, and so high above abstract general principles! She had not meant what she said. Her tongue was, after all, an unimportant part of her; her reasonings were absurd. She gazed at him like a wife, like a mother, like an angel, like a tantalising mystery. She said nothing. She gazed. And then she bent down and kissed him.

"Now, old lazybones!" the boy admonished his father.

"Johnnie!" his mother warned the boy. "Johnnie!"

The two males exchanged a glance. The fact was, Jack perceived that the boy understood his mother just as well as Jack himself understood her. The boy could not be misled by anything she said. The boy was as good a judge of character as anybody. Let her say what she chose—it couldn't matter. To worry about what she said would be childish.

Jack felt perfectly happy. The obsession of the evening and the long night was lifted from him, and he swam in a calm, fatigued felicity. Everything was right. The true colours of life were restored.

When it had been arranged that Jack should get up quickly, and the boy had gone to turn on the bath water, Jill said, very airily and sweetly, to Jack:

"I saw your silly old Snagge this morning, and he admitted I'd never said to him that you had decided not to exhibit this year. But he enjoys making trouble, I'm sure of that. Kiss me."

As he kissed her, Jack was thinking: "I wonder what sort of a night *she* had; but I shan't ask her. I wonder what really did pass between her and Snagge this morning; but I shan't ask her—or him either."

* * *

That same day, in his office, when he ought to have been conducting his business, Jack, amid yawns, was reflecting thus:

"I feel jolly tired, and I'm not doing my work properly. I've had a frightful time since yesterday afternoon. And really there's been no definite result. Jill and I haven't argued the thing out. The fact is, we stand just where we did before we had the row, except that I feel the difficulty of respecting a woman who goes on as Jill does at intervals. I was entirely innocent in the whole affair. I didn't ask for trouble. I didn't throw out any challenges. On the contrary it was I who was challenged, and I've been treated in a very underhand way. I've won on the point in dispute. We shall show chrysanths this year. But how about next year? Next year that woman will be capable of insinuating that because she behaved inexcusably this year and then gave in, therefore I ought to give in to her next year. No use reasoning! If I don't give in I shall be a brute, for she's the most persistent little minx that ever breathed.

"Of course, it's a trifle. And yet it isn't a trifle. I'm a bit of a feminist, and I'm all for justice; but these trifles are, in actual practice, far more important to me and to most men, and women too, than things like women's franchise, which I thoroughly believe in, or even than the reform of the divorce laws, which also I thoroughly believe in. The theoretical principles of reform are all very well. Nevertheless, I don't see exactly what reform is going to cure the periodical difficulties between husband and wife. Those are the root of the matter; you can call them trifles; still they're the root of the matter. I'm not perfect, Heaven knows, but nineteen times out of twenty the fault is Jill's.

"Is Jill worse than other women? No. Is she a good woman? Yes. Am I fond of her? Yes. Do I want to lose her? No. Should I be miserable if I did lose her? Yes. Is she 'decent'? Well, not always—at any rate, in my sense. That's the kernel. At intervals she will behave indefensibly. Dashed if I know what to do about it. All I know is that in this business of last night, for example, no unbiassed person could possibly say that I was in the wrong and that Jill wasn't in the wrong."

Thus Jack.

Well, "wrong" is perhaps a strong term to employ in the matter. We may admit that in regarding the quarrel as fundamental, and as of great practical importance to him and to Jill in its immediate effects, Jack was quite right. But we can safely say that in one particular he was at least unfortunate, if not stupid. He made no attempt to put himself in Jill's place, to make his brain work on the lines on which hers were working. An investigation of Jill's mental process might have caused him to adopt a different attitude. We must now approach Jill's brain.

CHAPTER NINE: FEMININE VIEW OF THE SEX DISCORD

CHAPTER NINE

FEMININE VIEW OF THE SEX DISCORD

In her private thoughts Jill, wife of Jack, held that the affair of Snagge (the head gardener) and the chrysanthemum show, though it might seem trivial enough to a man, was really important as illustrating the fundamental and incurable difficulties which a woman has with even the best husband. For her, it proved the impossibility of taking any male seriously, or at least of treating him, in your secret heart, as other than a child.

Jill was abroad in the beautiful garden early, Jack being characteristically asleep, and she happened to catch sight of Snagge fiddling around with his precious young chrysanthemum plants. It seemed as if he was about to re-pot them—and there were over a hundred of them.

Now, as Jill had just been noticing all kinds of things in the garden that urgently needed attention, the spectacle of Snagge devoting himself to fancy chrysanthemums annoyed her, for she divined that the ancient and obstinate Snagge had only one idea in his head—to take prizes at the chrysanthemum show. She did not like Snagge. He seldom smiled on her, and he never flattered her, and the alleged fact that he profoundly knew his job did not atone in her eyes for these defects. Worse, he always had an air of owning the garden and of treating the proprietors as unavoidable but regrettable trespassers. He had once gone so far as to be positively unpleasant because she had cut a few sweet-pea blossoms for herself. His argument was that he had been growing precisely those plants for a special purpose. What did it matter if he *had* been growing them for a special purpose? She was the mistress. She was dealing with her and Jack's blossoms, not Snagge's blossoms; any loss through her act would be their loss, not Snagge's loss; and she had resented his resentment.

Worse still, she was convinced that Snagge did what he liked with Jack; and she objected to any people, except herself, doing what they liked with Jack. Her instinct was always to protect Jack. The theory that men were the protectors of women seemed to Jill a sentimental falsity. Men protected women in unimportant physical and commercial matters; but in matters of consequence women were always the true protectors. And Jack, according to Jill's theory, needed to be protected against Snagge.

She suddenly decided to begin protecting him at once—and at the same time to put some salutary gloom into Snagge. Going up to Snagge, she said all in a breath:

"Good morning, Snagge, I think your master's made up his mind not to show chrysanthemums this year. That will give you more time to attend to the garden properly. But I expect he'll speak to you about it. You know I never interfere in the garden."

And she walked away, having no intention to argue with Snagge.

She had said something that was not true, because she was well aware that Jack had not decided not to show chrysanthemums. But it would be true in a few hours, for she intended instantly to persuade Jack to give up the show. Thus her very practical conscience was quite clear.

After lunch she started on Jack, remark-

constantly twitting her about her regard for "what people would say." You simply *had* to think, in the conduct of your life, about "what people would say," and Jack, in spite of his twittings, minded "what people would say" just as much as she did herself. But that he should bring this particular argument against her just now was outrageous. It was one more proof of the illogicalness of men, of their lack of grasp of realities. She would have none of the argument.

She did not want to quarrel, because in an hour or two the boy would be coming home for his holidays, and the day was a great day, but if Jack was so careless of the day as to behave as he was behaving—well, she couldn't help it: And if he was prepared, in his ruthless desire to win, to go quite close to the precipice of a row—well, she was prepared to go quite as close as he went.

When Jack, with his usual exasperating calmness, lit a cigarette and announced with his usual exasperating finality that she "must understand" that he had "decided" to let Snagge go in for the chrysanthemum show, her displeasure was complete. And her thoughts went out to the arriving boy. She

Silly expectation! Jack and the boy greeted each other with their usual surface display of callousness. She could have screamed. She very nearly did scream. But bravely she controlled herself, and said with restraint to Jack:

"Why do you *encourage* him to be so callous? This terrible callousness will be the death of me."

Herein was an appealing hint to Jack—which Jack ignored. And then, in the silence, she added:

"Johnnie, you really ought to show more respect for your father"—for Johnnie had greeted his father as offhandedly as he might have greeted a schoolmate. It was only their make-believe, of course, but she hated it. She wanted her two men to be exemplars of deportment and chivalry.

Jack said naught. Johnnie chucked her gently under the chin, and the touch of his boyish hand curiously thrilled her, so that she smiled in spite of herself. Tea passed off fairly well, and though Jack avoided saying anything directly to her, he was jovial enough, in his curt, hard way, with the boy.

Then the boy had to see his rearranged

and much-improved bedroom. The boy was very interested in his bedroom, and quite ready to go upstairs. Jill explained to the boy that his father had actually hung the pictures with his own hands! She laid emphasis on what Jack had done, and she had another foolish expectation—namely, that Jack would go upstairs with them. She did not ask him to do so, but she did everything short of asking him. Ask him she would not, fearing a rebuff. However, Jack did not go upstairs with them.

She had a good time with the boy upstairs. The boy approved the bedroom—was, in fact, delighted therewith. She made one or two slight alterations in it to please his strange whims. She went through all his clothes with him. She discussed all the practical details of school life, including especially the management of tuck-boxes and of pocket-money, and the character of the school matron. The boy expanded. She caressed him, and he was not restive under her caresses. His behaviour was quite different from what it would have been had his father been present.

Time slipped past like a dream. At last,

thinking of his duty to his father and anxious to bring these two close together, she sent him downstairs to his father, and remained behind to accomplish absurd little tasks which might have been left to the parlourmaid but which she would not leave to the parlourmaid. And while she was accomplishing these tasks she thought of the boy and his father downstairs, and hoped that they were achieving intimacy. And later she gave much trouble to the business of making herself very attractive for dinner.

At dinner she discovered, to her annoyance, that the boy had lost all his responsiveness and expansiveness. . . . Doubtless Jack's influence! He would not engage in general talk. He would not attempt to make general conversation, as a man ought. For her, the boy was already a man. She hated gaucherie and taciturnity, and the boy exhibited both defects. Jack, to do him justice, supported, in his curious, detached, rather unconvincing way, her exhortations to the boy.

But immediately afterwards Jack behaved very badly. During an awkward pause he broke out in that superior, irritating, chaffing, masculine manner of his and asked the boy:

"What were you and your mother plotting together upstairs?"

Plotting! She! She who was always so anxious to impress upon the boy the importance of his father, and to make the boy realise what he owed to his father in respect and deference! She who continually was trying, in regard to the boy, to do for the father what the father was too negligent to do for himself! She who, when she was enjoying the boy's company, had dismissed him so that he might be with his father! Plotting! Plotting against Jack, no doubt!

She controlled herself. She did not even bite her lip, nor turn pale, nor flush, nor let her eyes glint in anger. But she was nearly at the end of her self-control. And she felt in her inmost heart that her self-control was exhausted when the boy not merely helped himself to sugar in his coffee before offering the sugar to her, but omitted to offer the sugar to her after helping himself. She waited, with astounding patience. Neither of the men noticed that she was waiting. Jack ought to have corrected the boy; but he did nothing of the kind. She still waited, sugarless. And the unmannered lout, her son, sat careless on her right-hand stirring his coffee.

Her nerves gave way. She revolted against the whole masculine system. The public-school system was part of the masculine system, and here, in the person of her own lubber of a son, was the product of the public-school system! He could not or would not talk, and in a single term he had forgotten how to behave at table. And Jack sat brutally unconscious. She hated Jack, the terrible egoist, whose assumption of male superiority was implicit in every word and gesture of his life. Both Jack and his son were uncivilised. She alone stood for civilisation. She was determined to castigate the pair of them with one whip. She did not care what she did.

"Johnnie," she said, coldly and deliberately, "I'm waiting for the sugar. I wish you'd remember that you aren't at school. You're at home. You really must be more thoughtful for others. You're only a boy. Recollect that if your father never thinks of anybody but himself, that's no reason why you should be the same. Your father is your father."

Even in her icy anger against father and son she managed to put in a word to the son on behalf of the father. "Your father is your father."

* * *

It must surely have been apparent to any observer that Jack and Jill were now in the midst of a vast silent quarrel. Yet young Johnnie seemed to be quite indifferent to the obvious trouble; and this disturbed Jill still more, for it was further proof of the boy's horrid male callousness. She got him off to bed early, stating for the benefit of the public (the public being Jack) that he looked pale and tired. And she followed him upstairs. She was in two minds whether to come down again and have a big scene with her husband; but on the stairs she decided against this course, as involving a greater strain than she was equal to at the moment.

Half-way up the stairs she called out gently to Jack, who remained glowering in the drawing-room: "I shan't be down again, Jack. Good night." And Jack responded in a tone terrible and devastating, a murderous tone, an absolutely uncompromising tone: "Good night." It was just as if he had cried: "Curses upon you, wretch!"

In the boy's bedroom she indulged in no reproaches, either about behaviour at table or about callousness in general. She played the fond and somewhat martyrised mother, and she dawdled and gossiped and patted and tidied up and furtively caressed, and even answered the boy's jocularities with little jocularities of her own. She was very unhappy, but she was also very happy. At last she really had to leave the boy, who was yawning with his head on the pillow. She loathed the prospect of her own room and of the frightful, sleepless, worried night which she would certainly have to pass therein. And as she was crossing the landing she suddenly decided that she must not and could not go to bed without the big scene with Jack. It was a necessity of her nature that she should have the big scene. The scene might lead to nothing definite or useful, but it would give her the nervous relief which she so acutely needed. Thus she went back on her "Good night" to Jack and descended again to the drawing-room.

There he was lolling in an easy-chair, absorbed in the evening paper, as if nothing untoward had happened. He did not look up, but she gave him no chance to ignore her. She said at once, very calm and self-possessed, that she wanted to speak to him.

He cast the newspaper away in a fury, and bellowed back:

"Yes, and *I* want to speak to *you!*"

Oh! He was really angry. But what about? How ridiculous! How unreasonable! *He* had nothing to be angry about. He was doing exactly as he liked, as usual. However, she meant to be neither ridiculous nor unreasonable, and she gravely requested that he should let her speak. He glared, almost incandescent; and, fixing his eyes, she stated quite temperately her objection to being charged with "plotting." She showed how a charge of "plotting" could only be a charge that she plotted against him, and how the charge would cause the boy to think that she did not respect Jack's authority—which authority she was always upholding to the boy. In conclusion she offered a critical observation upon the merits and demerits of public schools, and a little half-apology for troubling Jack with her remarks.

The speech was admirably done. It was a rare instance of dignity and reasonableness. But Jack would not take it so! No, he was *determined* to be angry! He furiously flung at her that she knew perfectly well that his charge of plotting was only a joke! Well, if it was only a joke, the time for the joke had been very badly chosen. A new feeling came over her, and she felt that she simply did not care what happened. She was bitterly sarcastic about Jack's alleged joke, which she deemed to have been worse than his seriousness would have been. Jack went right on, his temperature ascending. "I suppose it was to strengthen my authority with the boy that you said I never think of anyone but myself!" he yelled. "A nice infernal lie to tell to the boy!"

So that was it. Her phrase had annoyed him. He was nursing it, chewing the cud of it and morbidly enjoying it! Well, she would not withdraw it, and she did not. It was true! It was true! In anything that really mattered he never did think of anyone but himself. She replied suitably, wounding him with skill, but at the same time making it quite clear that she was not complaining about Jack's egotism, nor denying that he was the most important person in the house—only she didn't want the boy to be like him. But Jack was far too excited to notice wounds. He proceeded, in ever-rising wrath: "And there's another thing! Why do you go and tell Snagge behind my back that I've decided not to exhibit chrysanthemums this year, when you know jolly well I haven't decided any such thing." Etc., etc., ending: "If I went into your kitchen and gave orders to your servants against your wishes I know what sort of a row there'd be. You must be mad!"

Now she fully understood. He must have been talking to Snagge early in the afternoon, and Snagge had told him what she had said to Snagge about him having practically decided not to exhibit. And that was why he had got angrier and angrier through the remainder of the day. She had a qualm. The fact was she had forgotten her little interview with Snagge. She admitted to herself that she had said something to Snagge that was not precisely accurate; but she had honestly meant to make it true. She had sincerely tried to persuade Jack to give up the show—only he would not listen to her. Besides, what, after all, *had* she said to Snagge? She had given no order to Snagge. On the contrary she had plainly conveyed to Snagge that the affair was in Jack's province and not in hers. True, Jack was supposed to be responsible for the garden, as she for the house; but did that mean that she must not open her mouth to Snagge? Assuredly not. Jack was continually opening his mouth to the indoor servants. Jack's grievance was preposterous. Moreover, old Snagge was a notorious mischief-maker, and Jack ought to have known better than to accept blindly the word of an employee when it involved his relations with his wife.

With a gesture she stopped Jack from bursting out afresh. She implored him not to get excited. She warned him that he was risking a sleepless night. She spoke her mind about Snagge, and she did not omit to assert positively—as, indeed, she was entitled to do—that she had given no orders to Snagge. Upon this she calmly retired. The tension of her nerves gradually slackened.

She undressed slowly, slipped into bed, and slept the long sleep of exhaustion.

* * *

The next morning she was awakened by a discreet tap at her bedroom door. It was early, and the housemaid had not yet paid her visit. "Come in," she murmured, and the boy came in. Evidently the boy had been up and about some time, and was bored in his solitude. "Pater's asleep," he said, sitting on the bed. "How do you know?" "Because I knocked at his door and he didn't answer; so I peeped in, and there he was fast asleep. Are you going to stay in bed all day, Mother? We have to get up at six-thirty at school—and I went to bed so early last night." She asked him to go into the garden, and said she would be with him in two jiffeys. "Jiffey" was the boy's own word. As she dressed she reflected upon Jack. She understood Jack's case. He had had a bad night—because of her—and now he was oversleeping himself, he who was always abroad long before there was any necessity to be abroad. Jack was just as much a child as Johnnie was a child. How absurdly he had behaved! How naughty he was! How unreasonable! How illogical! But he was not worse than other men. Perhaps he was better than most. He had frightened her a little last night by his fury. Never had she seen him quite so furious. She had not sufficiently made allowances for him. She had, indeed, been clumsy. If she did not succeed in twisting him round her little finger, the explanation could only lie in her clumsiness, for he was as simple as an infant! . . . Yet he could be extraordinarily subtle with her when he chose.

In the garden, and in the marvellous freshness of the morning, she found the boy talking to Snagge. She called to him from a distance: "Let's pick some flowers for Father, and then go and wake him." The boy took her arm. Before leaving the garden she found occasion to tell Snagge that he had wholly misunderstood her on the previous morning, and that Snagge's master was fully decided to exhibit chrysanthemums, *this year, at any rate.* Provided with flowers, which Jill had put into a glass, mother and son prepared themselves to capture the great being's bedroom. The door creaked horribly as Johnnie opened it, but there was no sound of voice or movement from the bed. "How tired he must be!" thought Jill. They both tiptoed into the room. The boy laughed and Jill could not help laughing because she felt so sure of herself. The boy had got the terrier under one arm, and now the animal leaped right into the bed. The invasion completed Jack's awakening. Jack gave a little exclamation in a tone that showed fatigue and the desire to be coddled. She placed the flowers by his side and her hand on his hot forehead and she looked into his eyes. She inquired of his eyes, and she smiled at him and yet pouted. Yes, he needed to be soothed, poor thing! Poor child! Poor old stick!

"Now, old lazybones!" the boy admonishingly greeted his important father.

"Johnnie!" she mildly protested against this lack of respect. The vast quarrel was over. Her white dress, her hand on his forehead, her smile, the flowers, the boy, had combined to bring it to an end. She was intensely happy. She could not comprehend why she had been unhappy. She lightly explained to Jack that the old fool Snagge had admitted giving misleading information to his master. " Kiss me!" she said imperiously. Jack kissed her. Millenial harmony was established.

* * *

That day, while Jack was reflecting upon the affair at his office, as I have previously recounted, Jill also was reflecting upon it. Their reflections differed in one detail, namely, that whereas Jack regretted that the altercation had not been argued out, as it were, and fought to a finish on logical lines, Jill had no such regret. Being a woman, she was far too practical to trouble about the way in which the difficulty had ended. It had been ended, and that was enough. Also, being a woman, she was far too much of a realist to dream that by any conceivable process of argument such altercations could be avoided in the future. She knew positively that altercations of a similar nature would recur, that they were inevitable. She agreed with Jack, however, that they were of fundamental importance and that the origin of them lay as the root of sex discord. She further agreed with Jack that the person at fault was the other person. She considered herself to be utterly innocent and victimised, as Jack also considered himself.

But she had the advantage over Jack in knowing that she, and not he, had brought the quarrel to a close. It was she who had made the final advance, which was equivalent to a surrender. It was she who first had consented to forgive and forget. (That Jack had temporarily carried his point about exhibiting chrysanthemums was a trifle—she meant to continue the campaign against flower-shows and to win it in the following year. She sincerely thought that the least Jack could do was to let her win it.) Why should she have to forgive and forget? Why was Jack, like all men, so queer and incomprehensible in his mental processes? Why was he such a child in really important matters? It was exceedingly unfair to women that men should be so. Men had all the material advantages, and yet they must needs seize the unfair advantage of behaving in a childish manner. However, she felt her deep superiority to Jack. She felt that she was his mother as well as his wife. . . .

In fine, she accepted the secret nature of things. Herein she was wrong, because there is no secret nature of things. She could never have thought exactly like Jack, but she might have made some attempt, by the exercise of imagination, to put herself in Jack's place and understand Jack's position. By so doing she might have helped to resolve part of the sex discord, which feminist legislation can never resolve unaided. But she did not do this. She did not try to do it. The notion of seriously doing it did not present itself to her. And thus she was no better than Jack—and no worse. In truth, she was very like him.

THE END

Printed in the United States
125114LV00005B/114/A

9 781430 478102